Dear Poo

Happy Christmas 2021
Thought you might like some tips.
Love
Tommo xxx

COFFEE FOR BEGINNERS:

The Ulimate Guide to Learn All You Need to Know About Coffee and His History

Jason Walters

© Copyright 2020 by Jason Walters - **All rights reserved.** This document is geared towards providing exact and reliable information in regards to the topic and issue covered. The publication is sold with the idea that the publisher is not required to render accounting, officially permitted, or otherwise, qualified services. If advice is necessary, legal or professional, a practiced individual in the profession should be ordered. - From a Declaration of Principles which was accepted and approved equally by a Committee of the American Bar Association and a Committee of Publishers and Associations. In no way is it legal to reproduce, duplicate, or transmit any part of this document in either electronic means or printed format. Recording of this publication is strictly prohibited and any storage of this document is not allowed unless with written permission from the publisher. All rights reserved. The information provided herein is stated to be truthful and consistent, in that any liability, in terms of inattention or otherwise, by any usage or abuse of any policies, processes, or directions contained within is the solitary and utter responsibility of the recipient reader. Under no circumstances will any legal responsibility or blame be held against the publisher for any reparation, damages, or monetary loss due to the information herein, either directly or indirectly. Respective authors own all copyrights not held by the publisher. The information herein is offered for informational purposes solely and is universal as so. The presentation of the information is without contract or any type of guarantee assurance. The trademarks that are used are without any consent, and the publication of the trademark is without permission or backing by the trademark owner. All trademarks and brands within this book are for clarifying purposes only and are owned by the owners themselves, not affiliated with this document.

TABLE OF CONTENTS

- Chapter 1: INTRODUCTION 5
- Chapter 2: THE COFFEE HOUSE HISTORY AND CAFE CULTURE 7
- Chapter 3: THE COFFEE HISTORY 16
- THE FIRST STEPS TO HARVESTING COFFEE 18
- THE AMERICANS & COFFEE 23
- THE REST OF THE WORLD & COFFEE ... 24
- COFFEE AND THE WORLD OF TODAY .. 26
- Chapter 4: THE GREEN COFFEE 28
- Chapter 5: THE DECAF COFFEE 36
- DECAF COFFEE HEALTH BENEFITS 38
- THE PROCESS 43
- Chapter 6: THE FILTER COFFEE 47
- HOW TO MAKE FILTER COFFEE 49
- Chapter 7: THE MOKA COFFEE 53
- THE MOKA POT 54
- STRENGTHS AND WEAKNESSES OF MOKA POT COFFEE 60
- Chapter 8: ESPRESSO 65
- THE HISTORY 65
- 10 FAMOUS DRINKS TO MAKE YOUR ESPRESSO MACHINE 77

MISUNDERSTANDINGS ON ESPRESSO.. 81
A COMPLETE LIST OF COFFEE DRINKS
OF EVERY TYPE 82
   Chapter 9: THE AMERICAN COFFEE 95
DRIP COFFEE vs POUR OVER 100
DRIP vs AMERICANO 102
DRIP COFFEE vs FRENCH PRESS 103
   Chapter 10: BARLEY COFFEE 105
THE ATTRIBUTES OF BARLEY COFFEE 112
   Chapter 11: GINSENG IN COFFEE 114
7 PROVEN BENEFITS OF GINSENG 118
   Chapter 12: ALCOHOL AND CAFFEINE 129
RECOGNIZING POISONING ALCOHOL .133
   Chapter 13: THE COLD BREW 135
CHOLESTEROL AND COLD BREW 139
9 IMPRESSIVE COLD-BREW COFFEE
BENEFITS 140
   Chapter 14: ARABICA COFFEE 157
BETWEEN DIFFERENCES THE BEANS ..159
ABOUT THE BEANS 160
ARABICA COFFEE BEANS TYPES 162
   Chapter 15: CONCLUSION 164

Chapter 1: INTRODUCTION

Coffee is one of the most sought after drinks in the world. Apart from water, some say it's the most commonly consumed substance in the world.

Yet coffee is more than just a drink. This is a vision, an excitement, a lifetime of moments of consoling gentle joy woven into our lives.

There is no question that the popularity of coffee as a beverage is due to both the caffeine it harbours and its sensory pleasure. Coffee lovers come to associate the caffeine's energizing lift with the beverage's richness and aroma which delivers it.

Coffee is produced from the seeds of a small red (sometimes yellow) fruit which grows between shrub and tree on plants halfway in size. The process of transforming these seeds into drinks is long and complex, perhaps the most complex process associated with any major drink.

This is also a very labour-intensive method involving a massive intercontinental partnership that begins with the coffee grower, travels from there to the picker, then to the mill workers who thoroughly harvest the fruit and dry the beans, then to those who clean and rate the beans, to those who roast them, to those consumers and baristas who eventually grind the beans and make the beverage.

Every act along the way can be done with either zeal and precision or careless shoddiness. It is the cumulative quality of all these creative contributions that together make the difference between a fine, distinctive cup and a fine cup.

Coffee Review promotes the fine, distinctive cup and praises its history and pleasures.

Chapter 2: THE COFFEE HOUSE HISTORY AND CAFE CULTURE

It's easy to get lost in the modern age of artisanal coffees and glossy-end machinery when thinking about the word "cafe." The aroma of freshly brewed French Roast and the velvety feel of soft couch cushions flood the mind, but cafe culture is more than just a pit stop for our daily joe cup.

Cafés are built around a few main components, with the successful selling of coffee and the people it brings in being two of the most popular. Like the coffee industry's deeply tangled web, cafes carefully balance the social, cultural, and economic motley that comes with both the drink itself and the complications of being a public sanctuary.

Coffee may be the product that gave rise to the institution, but its function was given to the company by the population filing through the cafe doors. While American cafes, starting in the mid-1960s, saw their origins with the second wave of coffee, cafes have far deeper roots than Starbucks or a 20-year-old mom-and-pop.

While coffee houses have changed in appearance and purpose over the years, they remain a staple in modern society.

Thanks to their significance in the social sphere and their ease of use, cafes rose to popularity in Europe during the late 17th century. Although restaurants and eateries specialized in meals, cafes limited their range in favour of coffee and inexpensive access for patrons. It made it especially available to the working class, to whom the institutions acted as a refuge to promote the society and facilitate the exchange of ideas and philosophy. This age became known as the Age of Enlightenment, as both a blessing and a curse.

Although many were provided with the opportunity to converse by the local alehouse, cafes remained a favourite confluence for the politically inclined, particularly those who did not have the forum or means to voice their misgivings elsewhere. Citizens upset by their new regime's upscaled pricing or legislation could find consolation in discussing these issues with their fellow cafe-goers. In an era of changing philosophies and moderate economic chaos, British cafes offered the unheard-of a voice and the freedom to discuss and host smart discourse that would otherwise have been drowned out under the establishment authority.

People of any social class could patronize the cafes; however, those in higher standing mostly avoided them for fear of losing rank. Earlier, they found cafes a nuisance. Cafes provided sanctum for their subjects and workers outside of their influence for the powers of the upper echelon, leaving space for the seeds of revolt to be planted and change.

This line of argument portrayed cafes as symbols of equality and justice, something that won them King Charles II's attention and eventual wrath, portraying the establishment as "a place where the disaffected meet and spread scandalous news about the actions of His Majesty and His ministers" to deter the congregation. His efforts had been fruitless.

Coffee houses were places where 17th-century traders met to do business—several banks and insurance companies formed from these buildings.

Cafes met their inevitable end due to the growing popularity of tea, following the rule of King Charles. British cafes, however, bred a generation of activists, authors, and musicians, setting the template for future coffee house culture.

Coffee houses and cafes' social and economic status made for a meeting place that was open to all people, irrespective of occupation. That wasn't just true in old Europe.

Bogota, Colombia, hosted many cafes around their sprawling cityscape in the mid-20th century. The popular culture of cafés was close to that of London, setting the groundwork for intersecting writers, activists and artists. Coffee was far from being exclusive to a coffee house, as the hub of a coffee-farming country. Coffee bars, coffee clubs, and even coffee pools were available.

The drink coincided with universal ideals and helped cross the mental and physical divide that would otherwise have divided people from different social classes. Like British coffee houses, men frequented those cafes after finishing their office work. Still, it was also a hub that gave equity to the property to musicians, journalists and authors, some doubling as galleries and convention centres. This, as in London, drew the attention of higher forces, to the tragic detriment of the Colombian cafes.

In addition to providing much-needed catharsis for working-class people, coffee houses provided the general public with a means of reconciliation and political revitalisation that eventually deepened the rift between parties in what would become the Colombian war. With the uprooted former militaristic forces clashing with some of the generation's brightest minds, it was hardly a secret that cafes posed a very serious threat to the increasingly dysfunctional government in Colombia. The dispute brought about the end of the national coffee house when significant rebellion erupted from the general public.

France is yet another prime example of the social and political cafe. Parisian cafes were hotbeds of thought, philosophy, and art in the 1900s, attracting people including Jean Cocteau, Ernest Hemingway, and F. Fitzgerald, Scott. During the Vietnam War, coffee houses in America were points of protest planning; a process later deemed "G.I. Cafes. "Although the gravity of the café culture has declined, artists and intellectuals remain cultural incubators.

In New York in the 1960s, coffee house culture was limited to Chock Full O'Nuts, a small supermarket that on a good day sold a modest cup of joe and muffin, and a few mom-and-pop shops that managed to retain post-Depression credibility. The definition of "coffee-house" has expanded in 2020 America.

New cafés that are most familiar appear to be commercial chains that grew in response to the second wave of coffee. Unlike British cafes, which used their population to grant the purpose of the café,

American cafes benefited from the capitalist mentality of the USA.

There's not one particular crowd associated with American cafes — the well-dressed businessman is frequenting them on his way to morning work as often as the screenwriter set up to work at the espresso bar.

Modern cafe culture is inextricably tied to the coffee industry it is built on, and as coffee changes, so is the American cafe. Instead of providing a united front for social conversation, coffee houses have become skilled in drawing a crowd based on the form of coffee they sell.

This means that the general business model has changed from one focused on the community to one focused on commodities which have helped revitalize the coffee industry as a whole.

Coffee is usually broken down into three primary waves. Although the 1960s made the most use of packaged, pre-ground coffee to mark the first coffee wave, the subsequent waves have moved from product to target.

In terms of their durability and style, American cafes have come to imitate tree rings from Seattle to Jacksonville. Take, for example, Starbucks and Tim Hortons. All chains rose to popularity in the 1990s to meet the need for speciality coffee beverages.

This included a variety of milky drinks based on espresso. Second wave cafes have become associated with easy access and mediocre coffee, with their commercial equipment and regional presence, as there is a contradictory focus on the consistency of the coffee.

The crowd looking for these cafes wants not just the elegant coffee drinks but also the comfort. Conveyor belt processes have made these beverages effective, if not especially inexpensive, in their manufacturing. That is what gives a fast remedy to the entrepreneurs, the students and those generally in need.

Third-wave café-goers don't share this ideology. Third-wave cafes emphasize the coffee itself, using modernized methods of identifying and sourcing quality coffee. His declaration of intent is to see coffee as "artisan food"—like wine — and patrons mirror this line of thought. Cafés like Blue Bottle, Birch, and La Colombe deliver quality beans to make premium coffee that doesn't have to be filled with milk and sugar to taste amazing. Unlike second-wave cafes that rely on seasonal flavours and marketing tactics to keep a crowd going, third-wave cafes use exclusivity as a means to maintain the interest of their patrons.

Third generations, therefore, are not looking to expand their culture so much as to attract people with similar values and interests.

You should remember that neither commercial-based wave offers affordability, but this does not stop either from being an enticing place for authors, musicians, and intellectuals to come together. Although cafe culture has evolved tremendously and changed, the core mandates — coffee, industry, and property — remain. With a range of sourcing and market for high-quality coffee at the forefront of our country's economy, don't be surprised if the coffee culture will continue to change in the years to come.

Chapter 3: THE COFFEE HISTORY

What's Coffee History? Why and when did we begin to drink the liquid gold? Today, many consider Coffee the essential fuel for a good, productive day.

Coffee history begins with a goat farmer living in Ethiopia. Coffee has spread across the globe to become one of the world's most consumed drinks.

But coffee itself has been through a few trials and tribulations since the discovery of its magical energy-giving properties centuries ago.

How did we transform a tiny, bright red coffee cherry into a drink that's consumed more than 2 billion times a day?

Here we will trace coffee on its journey, from its modest yet legendary origins in Ethiopia to how it became a world beverage, produced in more than 70 countries and drunk in every single country on the earth.

THE START OF COFFEE

According to legend-and, this is the most commonly cited story of the origin of a coffee-a goat herder named Kaldi, who lived on the Ethiopian plateau back in the 9th century, first noticed the energetic effects of the coffee bean.

One day Kaldi found that after some of his hearings had grazed on the coffee plant's bright red cherry, they seemed to possess boundless strength, his animals definitely more than the rest. As the story goes, as they had their bundles of energy bound all over the place, this left them too energized to fall asleep at night.

Kaldi tried the beans himself from here and found that they were still quite refreshing. He decided to share with the local monastery his discovery, which disregarded his anecdotes and threw the beans into the oven. A delicious scent quickly started to rise from the flames, and the beans were scraped out for further examination.

Afterwards, the monks decided to smash the beans and add them to the wash. They found, to their surprise and joy, that the beverage gave them the same strength and vigour it gave Kaldi and his goats, enabling them to remain awake and alert for the mass of the evening. Such monks transmitted their findings to other monks and monasteries, and so began the coffee journey!

The earliest copy we have of any text containing this tale is from 1671-seven hundred years after the truth- and this is why it is often quoted as a legend or myth. But all the same, it is a beginning!

THE FIRST STEPS TO HARVESTING COFFEE

It is important to note that there are other stories of coffee origin, and they all take place on the Ethiopian plateau, like the above. Modern technology and genealogical advances have allowed us to trace the coffee plant's origins back to Africa, and it is most probable, but not definite, that coffee originated from Ethiopia, and this is a consensus, often unquestioned.

No one is sure at what point people started to roast and brew coffee beans as we do today; although the above story says it, such a quick journey from coffee cherry to roasted cup of coffee is considered pretty unlikely.

Either way, the drink of coffee began to spread across the Arab peninsula and the Muslim world, with Yemen usually believed to be the first destination for coffees after they left Ethiopia. It had spread to the rest of the Middle East, Persia and Turkey by the end of the 16th century.

Until leaving the area, the Arabs held a monopoly on coffee production by either boiling, roasting, or baking the beans to ensure they did not germinate if planted. So how did coffee, which is now grown in over 70 countries, break the Arabs' monopoly on it?

EXPANDING THE COFEE

A man called Sufi Baba Budan smuggled out the first green or unroasted coffee beans that were smuggled away from their homeland, and the monopoly held on them by the Arabs.

He is honoured for this unique act of smugglers by both the Muslim and Hindu traditions (I believe that's a word), and is often portrayed with seven green coffee beans fastened to his chest; though some story accounts tell us, he hid them in his beard.

Sufi took those beans and planted them to be precise in his native India, in Mysore. It is from here that coffee is said to have spread throughout Europe before colonizers take it to their colonies and spread further afield.

THE ORIGINATION OF THE WORD: COFFEE

We talked about the origins of coffee, but where did the English word coffee come from? For most languages around the world, the word coffee has its version, and these are almost always along the lines of coffee or cafe, and all sound quite close to how we pronounce them for English.

The English version originated from the Dutch coffee, which originated from the Turkish kahve in turn, while the Turkish word came from the Arabic Mahwah. Both these terms have been Romanized, so you can see how our term coffee developed along the linage mentioned above, and its translations around the world.

But for what, coffee? Or, maybe we'd ask better, why qahwah? Originally this Arabic term described a wine, specifically a wine that was a suppressant of appetite; much like coffee. This is the most widely accepted version of why qahwah came to refer to the drink made from roasted and ground coffee beans.

THE FIRST DRINKERS

The first proof we have of people drinking coffee is through the Sufi monastery residential practices-Sufi is known as "Islamic Mysticism"- to help keep them awake for the mass of the evening. Coffee spread to Mecca from here though its use was not limited to monasteries.

Coffee houses started popping up in the region, and they were places where men would get together to drink coffee, discuss the day's issues, and smoke hookah. Coffee has also been served as a symbolic gesture of kindness and hospitality in the homes, inviting someone else into their house.

As coffee came to Europe, life started, as did any new international import, as a luxury commodity exclusively for the continent's rich and noble citizens.

However, coffee spread rapidly throughout society, and after a coffee trade had been established, public coffee houses emerged in many cities. In these coffee houses, particularly in Europe, anyone could come in as long as they could afford a cup of coffee in a get.

Once we continue explaining the impact that the coffeehouse had on culture, we will see how coffee first arrived in Europe and how the Europeans introduced it to the rest of the world.

THE INCREASE IN COFFEE POPULARITY

From Ethiopia and the Arab peninsula coffee spread to northern Africa, Turkey and from there it made its way to Europe, its first port of call being Venice; a port which conducted an enormous amount of trade with North Africa and the Middle East.

It was introduced to the wealthy Venetians by merchants arriving there, and they enjoyed it. As imports grew from here, prices fell, and availability increased.

Coffee was first regarded as a "Muslim drink," and then cautioned against consumption by Italian Christians. However, after it was consumed and declared a "Christian beverage" by Pope Clement VII, it was generally accepted into society; before this, there were many attempts in Italy to prohibit coffee outright.

It is worth remembering here that coffee was banned on two occasions across the Arabian peninsula in the early 1500's-about 100 years before coffee reached European shores- due to its calming effects.

While coffee spread and made its way into Europe's wealthiest homes, it would not take off as a worldwide beverage until the Europeans first started selling it to their home countries from their colonies in India.

LARGE SCALE EXPORT OF COFFEE

After colonizing large parts of India the Dutch, followed by the British, started importing large amounts of coffee back to their homeland. Previously, countries on the Arabian peninsula had a coffee trade monopoly and charged very high prices for their product.

The new products now arriving in Northern Europe helped to lower prices and increase the supply of this exotic beverage.

When supply had improved, and wealthier Europeans had acquired a taste of this beautifully relaxing beverage, demand soared, and the hunt for the coffee tree began.

The Dutch won the coffee tree race and got some growth in the Amsterdam Botanical Gardens in the early 1600s. By the mid-1600s the trees thrived, and some were brought out to be planted in their colonies in southern India and Ceylon, Sri Lanka of today.

These sights were soon abandoned, and the Dutch transferred their plantations to their outposts in Indonesia and Suriname. These colonies became Europe's main supplier of coffee within a few years.

The Netherlands, becoming the sole owners of the coffee tree in Europe, gave the French King as a gift as they signed a treaty clipping from one of their bushes.

Sometime later, a Frenchman, Gabriel de Clieu, persuaded the King's gardener to send him a clipping of this vine, which he had transported to a French Caribbean region. In Gabriel's own words, we find an account that tells us that for a period of this trip, water was rationed, and he shared his portion with his precious cargo.

He also tells how at least one attempt to sabotage the plant had to be thwarted. In the Caribbean, the coffee tree thrived, so much, so that much of the coffee plants found in South America, Central America, and Mexico derived from this clipping.

THE AMERICANS & COFFEE

Coffee has had a major influence on the American countries and is considered to this day one of the region's most valuable crops. It's also that about 600 million people worldwide depend for their existence on the coffee industry; that's around 10 per cent of the world population. Yet let's digress.

Coffee production in the Americas relied heavily on the work of African slaves and conquered the indigenous peoples. It is this use of slave labour that is attributed to the success of France in the Caribbean, and the abundance of coffee throughout America's tropical region.

Brazil is now the top growing nation in the world for coffee, by a wide margin. Throughout Brazil, however, coffee was not planted until the early 1700s. While it was a common plant, it did not gain popularity until after Brazil gained its independence in the early 1800s.

Then, Brazil's new rulers cleared huge swaths of land for coffee cultivation. It is because of this that Brazil became the world's largest coffee producer by 1852. A title it's been holding ever since.

In 1774, and as a result of the Boston Tea Party events of 1773, John Adams, one of the founding fathers of the USA, said that tea would be "universally renounced" and many Americans turned to drink coffee, believing that consuming tea was now quite unpatriotic.

THE REST OF THE WORLD & COFFEE

The Dutch introduced coffee to large parts of Asia and contributed to export and production in India, Indonesia and Japan. Notably, it was a Spanish monk who brought coffee to the Philippines where coffee cultivation and export thrived until about of coffee rust, combined with an infestation of insects, killed many of its crops in the late 1880s.

After this big dip growth, the Philippine coffee company has been swallowed up by Brazil's coffee giant.

Coffee may have started its story in Ethiopia, but it never really took off in the region. True, coffee now accounts for around 25 per cent of global exports, but it was not commonly grown in the original home of the world's third most popular beverage before the last century.

COFFEE AND THE CAFETERIA

As mentioned before, coffee and the coffee house's popularity spread throughout Europe, as supply followed suit. In the Middle East, coffee and coffee shop culture began, and it seems that wherever coffee was drunk — but not where it was grown — coffee houses followed quickly in its wake.

Such coffee houses started to play an important role in society and became places where people could go to socialize, discuss the news of the day, watch live music and play games.

Coffeehouses across Europe and the Middle East gained nicknames such as "penny universities" in England-where it was said that one could be educated for the value of a penny equal to the price of a cup of coffee or in the Middle East where they were called "schools of the wise."

During the enlightenment period of the late 1600s coffeehouses were the epicentres of, developments in science, and evolving thinking in England and France, enabling people to discuss and coordinate their revolutionary thoughts and ideas in a free meeting place.

The change in religious opinion and the new ideas that arose from the meetings that took place in coffee houses during this period were so detrimental to the general standard and way of thinking that England's King Charles II attempted to shut them down in 1675; this, luckily, failed.

Coffeehouses across the United States are a relatively new phenomenon, not having become mainstream meeting places until around 60 years ago. Some musicians, but mainly churches and groups increased their popularity as informal locations where they could hold meetings.

COFFEE AND THE WORLD OF TODAY

From the advent of coffee as beverage coffeehouses, they have existed and supplied people of all groups and educational levels. Space where everyone was on a level footing and where there was none of the unruly nature found in bars and pubs; in fact, alcohol was banned to prevent such disturbances.

Even today, coffeehouses around the world are seen as comfortable first-date settings, meeting friends you haven't seen, working, and studying in a long time.

Whereas in coffeehouses, people used to work with each other today use the internet to collaborate with others across the globe; maybe in coffeehouses too.

Coffee is considered a drink for breakfast, and this is due to its well-known stimulating properties. Some say that once they have had their morning coffee cup, they "are not awake."

In all the far corners of the world, on vessels, on planes and even in space, coffee can be found and drank. Coffee is constantly battling beer with both of these lining up behind water and tea for the position of "the world's third famous beverage."

The tale of coffee started in Ethiopia, and its development is closely intertwined with the rise of the colonial powers in Europe. Having endured prohibitions, persecution, a beard trip and a water-rationed transatlantic trip coffee are now one of the world's biggest exports, and about 10 per cent of the world's population can rely on themselves as part of the coffee industry worldwide.

All from a few cherries on the Ethiopian plateau that energized some goats over 1100 years ago.

Chapter 4: THE GREEN COFFEE

Green coffee is just raw, unroasted beans. Proponents claim that a variety of health benefits offer green coffee, green coffee extract, and green coffee supplements. While used primarily for weight loss, green coffee may help regulate blood sugar and improve memory and cognitive skills in older adults.

Through herbal medicine, it is claimed that green coffee helps to treat the following health conditions:

- Alzheimer's disease
- Diabetes
- Colorectal cancer
- High blood pressure
- Metabolic syndrome
- Heart disease
- Parkinson's disease
- Obesity

It is also said that green coffee promotes weight loss, reduces inflammation and slows the ageing process. Through studies, some of the arguments are better backed than others.

Medical Care

Green coffee contains chlorogenic acid, a potent antioxidant that appears to break down when roasted with coffee beans. Some research suggests chlorogenic acid retention in green coffee is largely responsible for health benefits[1].

While there is a limited study, there is evidence that green coffee can improve metabolism (conversion of calories and oxygen into energy). Metabolism does not only imply digestion; it dictates how well all of the body's cells function, including those of the heart, lung, kidney, liver and brain.

Here's just a sample of what current research is saying about green coffee 's benefits:

Energy loss

According to a review of studies published in Gastroenterology Research and Practice,[2] of the three clinical trials included in the review, each revealed that green coffee extract was significantly more effective than placebo in reducing body weight.

While the researchers admitted that the studies were poorly designed, they concluded that there was sufficient congruence to suggest that green coffee is a safe and potentially beneficial aid to weight loss.

A 2013 study of research published in the Integrative Medicine Review of Evidence went much further.

The researchers stated in their study of five clinical trials and one meta-analysis that, as a result of green coffee extract, people lost about 1 kilogram (kg) to 8 kg of body weight — or around 2 to 17 pounds.

As with the study in 2011, the findings have been constrained by the relatively low nature of the studies studied.

Diabetes Diagnosis

Another of the most common polyphenols in the foods we consume is chlorogenic acid. Polyphenols are antioxidant compounds present in plants. Not only are they fighting free radicals which damage cells, but they are also believed to help regulate blood sugar (glucose).

A 2010 study recorded that chlorogenic acid administered at a dose of 5 mg/kg of body weight could normalize glucose levels in diabetic rats4.

According to research from Australia in 2009, daily consumption of three to four cups of decaffeinated coffee containing high concentrations of chlorogenic acid reduced the risk of type 2 diabetes by 30 per cent in humans.

Although green coffee, which has higher levels of chlorogenic acid, is believed to provide even greater protection, this has yet to be confirmed in science.

High pressure on the blood

There is evidence that green coffee can reduce blood pressure. According to a 2006 Japanese study, green coffee extract prescribed for 12 weeks at 140 mg daily reduced systolic blood pressure by five mmHg and diastolic blood pressure by three mmHg in mildly hypertensive adults5.

This does not mean that green coffee will benefit everyone with high blood pressure, although it is encouraging. It is especially true for those with a sensitivity to caffeine in whom green coffee can cause the same symptoms as regular coffee, including elevated blood pressure.

Interestingly, none of the Japanese trial participants experiences any weight or body mass changes.

Alzheimer's Disease

Green coffee may avoid or reduce some of the cognitive and neuropsychiatric symptoms of Alzheimer's disease, as far-fetched as it may seem.

Chlorogenic acid has a weak stimulating effect, approximately one third as potent as caffeine. While it does not offer nearly the same "shake" as caffeine elsewhere, it can boost moods, with less chance of jitteriness or irritability.

Animal studies indicate green coffee can boost both brain function and mood. According to a 2012 study in Nutritional Neuroscience, green coffee extract's antioxidant properties have helped to retain normal brain metabolism in mice compared to mice that were not given the extract.6 Declines in brain metabolism are key indicators of Alzheimer's risk.

A 2017 review of studies echoed these claims, suggesting that the green coffee extract soothes the brain's oxidative stress as "neuroprotective." Future research is likely to measure how robust this protection can be.

Neurodegenerative diseases such as Parkinson's disease can receive the same benefits.

Colorectal Cancer

The benefits of green coffee in the prevention of colorectal cancer are even less obvious.

On the one hand, animal studies have long demonstrated how coffee polyphenols can help protect against colon tumour formation.7 It has been suggested that green coffee, which is composed of 14 per cent chlorogenic acid, can enhance this effect.

On the flip side, coffee contains compounds that can increase the risk of colorectal cancer, either by encouraging cell mutation or by causing cellular DNA breakdown. It is not yet clear if these carcinogenic compounds are produced during the roasting of the beans.

Ultimately, these competing powers do not tend to encourage or discourage colorectal cancer from growing. With green coffee, it would be fair to conclude the same before research might prove otherwise.

Potential adverse effects

Extracts of green coffee and black coffee are usually considered healthy for adults. That said, little is known about green coffee extract or supplements' long-term health.

As with regular coffee, green coffee, particularly those with sensitivity to caffeine, may cause side effects. Including:

- Insomnia8
- Irritability
- Nervousness
- Stomach upset8
- Increased heart rate
- Nausea
- Ringing in the ears (tinnitus)
- Headache

There is some concern that long-term or excessive green coffee consumption may increase the risk of homocysteinemia (the excessive amino acid accumulation of homocysteine associated with heart disease and miscarriage).

There are no known interactions with green coffee on drugs.

Preparation and Dosage

There is no recommended standardized dosing of green coffee extracts or supplements. In general, terms, if only to avoid side effects, it is best to stay within the recommended dose on the product label.

How to Bring

There are many natural food stores and several grocery stores where you can find green coffee. Many of them come in single-serving packets. Unlike regular coffee, the aroma and flavour of which are the result of roasting, green coffee has a slightly bitter taste and is almost entirely without aroma.

Green coffee extracts and supplements can be found online as well as in food aid specialist stores. Some of the extracts are packed as tinctures which you use a dropper to take. Others come in formulas with a tablet or gel seal.

It's important to note that supplements are mostly unregulated in the United States.9 Consistency and dosage variations between one brand and the next may be major.

Select only supplements tested and approved by a recognized certifying body such as the USA to ensure safety and quality. NSF International Pharmacopeia (USP), and ConsumerLab.

Other Questions

You may also make a green coffee drink instead of taking vitamins or extracts. To do this, grin a coffee grinder with two ounces of raw beans. (The beans don't grind quickly, so there will be big chunks.) Simmer for 15 minutes in 12 ounces of water, then let steep for an hour before straining. Avoid adding sugar when used as a weight loss aid.

Although the taste is too bitter for most people, it can be blended with daily roasted coffee. Green coffee beans on the plus side contain 20 per cent of the caffeine found in roasted beans (approximately 20 mg versus 100 mg per cup, respectively).

Chapter 5: THE DECAF COFFEE

For decaffeinated coffee Decaf is short.

It is coffee from coffee beans which have removed at least 97 per cent of their caffeine. There are several methods of collecting caffeine from coffee beans. They are mostly water, carbon dioxide or organic solvents. Coffee beans are washed in the solvent until the caffeine is absorbed from it and the solvent is removed afterwards.

You may also extract caffeine using carbon dioxide or a charcoal filter — a procedure known as the Swiss Water CycleThe beans are decaffeinated before being roasted and soiled. In addition to the caffeine content, decaf coffee's nutritional value would be nearly equal to regular coffee.

The taste and smell can get a little milder, however, and the colour can change depending on the process used. To those that are sensitive to the bitter taste and scent of standard coffee, this may make decaf coffee more appealing.

Decaf coffee beans are washed in solvents before roasting to eliminate 97 per cent of the caffeine content. Apart from the caffeine, decaf coffee's nutritional value would be almost equivalent to standard coffee.

How much coffee is in Coffee Decaf?

1. The decaf coffee is not completely free of caffeine.
2. This does also contain varying levels of caffeine, typically about 3 mg per cup.
3. One research found that every cup of decaf (6 oz or 180 ml) contained 0–7 mg of caffeine
4. At the other hand, an average daily cup of coffee contains around 70–140 mg of caffeine, depending on the form of coffee, method of preparation and cup size (4).
5. So, while decaf isn't entirely free of caffeine, the amount of caffeine is typically very low.
6. Decaf coffee is not free from caffeine, as each cup contains about 0–7 mg. This is much less, however than the amount found in a standard coffee.
7. Decaf coffee is loaded with nutrients and antioxidants

Coffee is not the villain it was made to be.

It is, in reality, the single greatest source of antioxidants in the Western diet. Decaf typically contains antioxidants comparable to standard coffee, but they may be up to 15 per cent lower

The most likely cause of this disparity is a slight loss of antioxidants during the decaffeination cycle.

Hydrocinnamic acids and polyphenols are the principal antioxidants in regular and decaf coffee.

Antioxidants, called free radicals, are very effective in neutralizing reactive compounds.

This reduces oxidative damage, which can help prevent heart disease, cancer, which type 2 diabetes diseases. Aside from the antioxidants, decaf also contains small quantities of other nutrients.

One cup of brewed decaf coffee contains 2.4% of the required daily magnesium intake, 4.8% of potassium and 2.5% of niacin, or vitamin B3

This may not sound like a lot of nutrients, but when you drink 2-3 (or more) cups of coffee a day, the quantities add up quickly.

Decaf coffee contains antioxidants which are similar to standard coffee. These primarily contain chlorogenic acid and other polyphenols. Decaf coffee also contains several small amounts of nutrients.

DECAF COFFEE HEALTH BENEFITS

The fact is, despite being demonized in the past, the coffee is healthy for you.

It is related to various health benefits, due primarily to its antioxidant content and other active substances.

Yet it can be hard to assess the precise health effects of decaf coffee.

This is because most studies measure the consumption of coffee without distinguishing between standard and decaf coffee, and some don't even have coffee decaf.

Most of those studies are also observational. We can't say that coffee brought the advantages, just that they are correlated with consuming coffee.

Type 2 Diabetes, work in the liver and premature death

Both daily and decaf consuming coffee have been linked to a decreased risk of type 2 diabetes. Could cup every day will reduce the risk by up to 7 per cent

This indicates that other than caffeine components may be responsible for certain protective effects

Decaf coffee 's effects on liver function are not as well known as standard coffee's. Nonetheless, one major observational study linked decaf coffee to reduced levels of liver enzymes, indicating a protective effect

Drinking decaf coffee was also related to a minor but substantial reduction in the risk of premature death, as well as stroke or heart attack death

Decaf coffee will lower the risk of type 2 diabetes. This may also reduce the chance of untimely death.

Ageing and developing neurodegenerative disorders

All daily and decaf coffee appear positive for age-related mental decline

Studies of human cells also show that decaf coffee can protect neurons in the brain. This could help prevent neurodegenerative diseases such as Alzheimer's and Parkinson's disease from developing

One study suggests this could be due to the coffee chlorogenic acid, rather than caffeine. But caffeine itself was also associated with a reduced risk of dementia and neurodegenerative diseases

Some studies indicate that people who drink regular coffee are at lower risk for Alzheimer's and Parkinson's, but more detailed studies are needed on decaf.

Decaf coffee will protect against mental deterioration due to ageing. This may also reduce the risk of illnesses such as Alzheimer's and Parkinson's.

Reduced heartburn symptoms and reduced rectal cancer risk

A common side effect of coffee-drinking is heartburn or acid reflux.

It is something that many people feel, and drinking decaf coffee will alleviate its unpleasant side effect. Decaf coffee has been shown to produce far less acid reflux than regular coffee.

Drinking two or more cups of decaf coffee a day was also associated with up to 48 a cent lower rectal cancer risk.

Decaf coffee induces much lower acid reflux than standard coffee. I am drinking more than two cups a day can also lower rectal cancer risk.

THERE ARE SOME BENEFITS OF REGULAR COFFEE OVER DECAF

Coffee is perhaps better known for its influence on stimulants.

It increases alertness and reduces feelings of exhaustion.

These effects are directly associated with the stimulant caffeine, which is naturally found in coffee.

The caffeine is specifically related to some of the beneficial effects of standard coffee, and decaf does not have such effects.

Here are some advantages which will probably only apply to regular coffee, not to decaf:

- Improved mood, reaction time, memory and mental function.
- Improved fat burning and metabolism
- Athletic performance improved
- Reduced risk of mild depression and women with suicidal thoughts
- Much lower risk of liver cirrhosis or liver damage in the final stages.

It is worth noting. However, that daily coffee research is much more comprehensive than what is available for decaf coffee.

Regular coffee provides various health benefits which do not apply to decaf. Those include better mental health, increased metabolic rate, increased success in sports, and a lower risk of liver damage.

Who would have Over Standard Coffee Decaf?

When it comes to caffeine tolerance, there is a lot of human variation.

One cup of coffee can be excessive for some people, while this maybe six or more cups for others.

Excess caffeine in sensitive individuals can overload the central nervous system, causing restlessness, anxiety, digestive issues, heart arrhythmia or difficulty sleeping.

People who are highly sensitive to caffeine might want to limit their regular coffee intake or switch to decaf or tea.

Caffeine-restricted diets may also be required for those with certain medical conditions. This involves patients taking prescription drugs which can interfere with caffeine.

Also, pregnant women and women who are breastfeeding are advised to limit their intake of caffeine. Kids, teenagers and individuals with anxiety or sleeping problems are also encouraged to do so.

To people susceptible to caffeine, decaf can be a suitable alternative to standard coffee. Pregnant women, adolescents and individuals taking certain medicines may also want to opt for decaf rather than regular.

Coffee is one of the Planet's healthiest drinks.

It is loaded with antioxidants and linked to a reduced risk of serious diseases of all kinds.

Not all should drink coffee, however, and in some people, the caffeine should cause problems.

Decaf is an ideal way to enjoy coffee for these men but without the side effects of unnecessary caffeine.

Decaf has the same safety benefits for everyone with none of the side effects.

THE PROCESS

"In 1905 Ludwig Roselius invented the first decaffeinating method for coffee. Roselius' method used benzene, a potentially toxic hydrocarbon, to remove caffeine from pre-moistened, green coffee beans. Modern processes of decaffeination are much more gentle; many point this out by claiming to be 'naturally decaffeinated.'

"There are currently three major processes in use for decaffeination. We may have some basic differences. The green or roasted beans are first moistened in all three approaches, thus making the caffeine soluble so it can be drawn out.

We all decaffeinate green coffee at low temperatures, usually between 70 and 100 degrees centigrade (160 to 210 degrees Fahrenheit).

"One approach is water processing. As you would imagine, this procedure uses water as a solvent to remove caffeine from green coffee beans. Usually, eight to 12 vessels are used to extract batteries; each vessel holds green coffee at a different decaffeination level.

"A mixture of water and green-coffee extract, which has already been reduced in caffeine, circulates around the coffee beans inside the extraction battery (oils in the coffee extract aid during the decaffeination process), isolates and empties the vessel which has been exposed to low-caffeine extract after a predetermined period.

The vessel exposed to the low-caffeine extract shall be isolated and drained. Then the decaffeinated coffee beans are rinsed and dried, and a vessel that contains fresh green coffee is put on the water. The caffeine-rich extract from the vessel containing the fresh, green coffee is passed through an activated charcoal bed that absorbs the caffeine.

This charcoal was pretreated with a carbohydrate, usually, saccharose, which helps to absorb caffeine without eliminating any other compounds that contribute to the coffee's flavour. The sucrose blocks carbon sites from the hot, green-coffee extract that would usually absorb sugars. The extract that in caffeine can then be reused to continue the cycle anew. The water process is natural (that is, no chemicals are involved), but it is not very specific to caffeine; it removes 94 to 96 per cent of caffeine.

"The second method of decaffeination is the direct solvent method. Nowadays, this technique usually uses methylene chloride (used mainly in Europe), coffee oil or ethyl acetate to dissolve the caffeine and extract it from the coffee. Ethyl acetate is an ester found naturally in fruits and vegetables such as bananas, apples and coffee.

The liquid solvent is circulated through a layer of wet, green coffee beans, extracting some of the caffeine, then retrieving the solvent in an evaporator and cleaning the beans with water. Solvent traces are extracted from the coffee by steaming the beans to trace amounts.

This process also uses batch processing-that is, the solvent is applied to the pot, circulated and drained several times before the coffee is decaffeinated to the desired amount. Solvents are used because they are usually more specifically aimed at caffeine than charcoal, with almost all noncaffeine solids left behind. The more caffeine-specific solvents, such as methylene chlorides, will remove caffeine from 96 to 97 per cent.

"The third approach, supercritical carbon dioxide decaffeination, is very similar to direct solvent methods, except that in this case, the solvent is carbon dioxide. High-pressure vessels (operating at approximately 250 to 300 times atmospheric pressure) are used to circulate carbon dioxide through a bed of pre-moistened, green coffee beans.

Carbon dioxide takes on special, 'supercritical' properties at these pressures that improve its utility as a solvent. Supercritical carbon dioxide has a liquid-like density, but its viscosity and diffusiveness are close to that of a gas. These attributes decrease their pumping costs significantly.

Carbon dioxide is a common solvent because it has a critical point of relatively low pressure, and of course, it is plentiful. The carbon dioxide-rich in caffeine that exits the extraction vessel is either channelled through an activated charcoal bed or through a water 'bath' tower to absorb the caffeine. The carbon dioxide is then recirculated back into the tank for retrieval. Supercritical decaffeination of carbon dioxide is capital-intensive, but it provides very good yields. It can usually remove 96 to 98 per cent of the caffeine that was originally in the beans.

Chapter 6: THE FILTER COFFEE

Filter Coffee is South India's best-known coffee. Let's see how coffee came to India, and it became the most loved filter coffee in South India.

A brief tale about how coffee came to India

For many Indians, there are few caffeinated drinks that prove as potent and satiating as a cup of good old filter coffee. Brewed extra hard with loads of sweetened milk and served in steel cups on top of containers called dabarah, this local coffee has been fueling parts of South India for centuries now. Hold on reading to learn everything about South Indian coffee filter.

Coffee arrives in India

India's coffee experiment is said to have its origins in Karnataka in the early 17th century. Baba Budan, a Chikmagalur Muslim saint, is said to have smuggled seven coffee beans from present-day Yemen as he returns from Hajj or a pilgrimage to Mecca. Throughout the time, exporting green coffee beans from the Arabian Peninsula was illegal, as local coffee farmers and traders decided to maintain their monopoly. Nevertheless, not only did Baba Budan manage to sneak them into India by hiding the beans in his beard, but he was also able to plant them in the

Chandragiri Hills district of Chikmagalur, where they were soon to grow.

Though production of coffee continued well over a century later in the Chandragiri Hills, it is estimated to have been mostly restricted to the region. It was only in the 19th century that coffee plantations were built to export the yield. Regardless, coffee had become enormously popular throughout the southern states of Karnataka, Tamil Nadu, Andhra Pradesh and Kerala by the 20th century.

Popularity increase

As the British developed their rule in India, they came across the coffee culture of South India, too, and took it upon themselves to market their products. Throughout the hills of Wayanad in northern Kerala, Coorg in southern Karnataka and other regions coffee plantations became widespread under these efforts. While the yield was mostly exported, at that time also a local market was developing.

South Indians have started brewing their coffee with milk at some point in the 19th century, and then sweetening it with honey or jaggery. Although by the late 19th century it was a regular requirement in many southern homes, coffee was still an uncommon occurrence in the northern half of the country. It was during the mid-20th century that the establishment and spread of the famous Indian Coffee House bridged this divide.

The invention of coffee houses has replaced earthen pots used to brew and serve coffee with stainless steel tumblers – synonymous with Indian filter coffee to this day. The tumbler has two parts, which resemble cylindrical cups, one of which is poured on fresh ground and then squeezed (like a French press) while the other half gathers the coffee that has been brewed.

During the 20th century, its influence soared across the world, but it also spread outwards – to Malaysia and Singapore. Identified as kopi Tarik, the drink was introduced via roadside stalls run by communities of Indian migrants.

HOW TO MAKE FILTER COFFEE

1. This picture is from coffee filter from South India. It's coming in various sizes. The one I have serves 2 to 3 (glasses) tumblers

2. Such are the parts. It is composed of 2 cylindrical vessels. It has perforations within the top vessel. The top vessel fits into the lower vessel that stores the brew of coffee. The top vessel is often followed by a pressing disk with a handle and a lid.
3. It is a top-vessel image with the perforations.

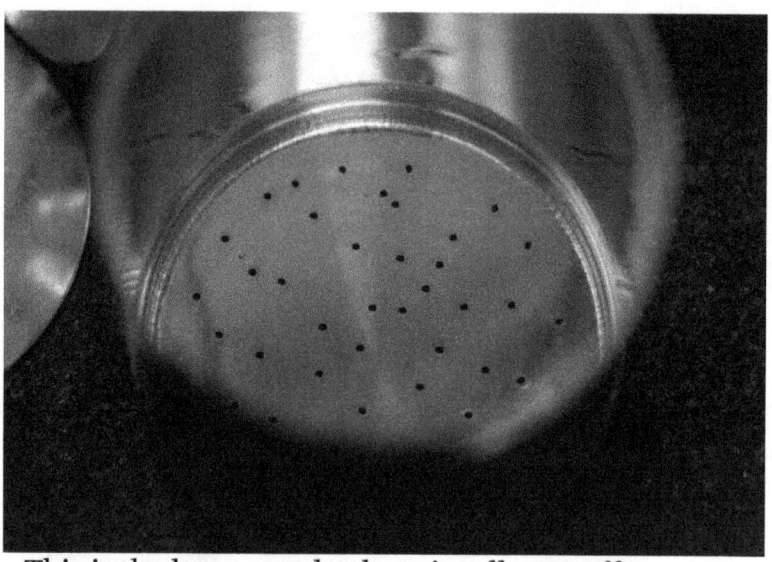

4. This is the base vessel, where it collects coffee decoction.
5. Now get to the coffee. Use ground coffee to prepare Coffee Filter. Fits the top of the bottom vessel.

Now take three teaspoons of coffee and put it with the perforations in the top vessel. I use the following proportions for the filter I do have:

- Four teaspoons of coffee powder-a strong coffee
- Three teaspoons-average solid
- 1.5 to 2 spoonfuls – light coffee

6. Spread the coffee powder gently and even out with your fingers or with a small spoon.

7. Place the handle onto the coffee powder with the pressing disk.

8. Heat 1 cup of water in a pot of sauce, and let it boil.

9. Upon boiling the water gently pour the water into the top dish.

10. Fill it to 3/4 or nearly complete. The top vessel was nearly full of hot water, as I used 1 cup.

11. Fill with fabric. Wait in the lower vessel for 10 to 12 minutes, until the coffee decoction percolates.

12. A bit of water is still left here on this photo.

13. All of the coffee is roasted in the picture below. Cover and hang on.

14. After brewing all of the coffee, heat 3/4 cup full fat or whole milk until it gets hot and boils. Only before all the water percolates, you can also start heating milk.

15. Now take a tumbler (glass) and bring in 2 teaspoons of sugar.

16. Put 1/4 to 1/3 cup of hot boiling milk directly into the tumbler and strain.

17. To avoid the malai that comes with the boiling milk, I strain the milk. You can add milk if you like malai, without straining it. You can add as much or less milk according to your preference.

18. Now pour ¼ of the brewed coffee or ⅓ of the cup. You can add as much or as little, as you want.

19. So here the coffee filter is ready, but before you savour it, a few steps forward.

20. Now take Dabarah, or This is a tiny pan shaped vessel used to cool the coffee. The coffee is poured from the tumbler to the Dava, and so on. And the sugar dissolves, forming a top layer of foam on the coffee. Pour the coffee from the tumbler into the Dava from a height.

21. Now pour the Dava coffee back into the tumbler.

22. Repeat pouring coffee from the tumbler back into the Davara and vice versa. This operation, you can do 2 to 3 times. Don't overdo it as the coffee gets cold then. If you wish, you can even skip that step.

23. Serve hot Coffee Cover. It must be served right away as soon as it has been made.

Chapter 7: THE MOKA COFFEE

Origin of the Moka Pot

With lots of energy, many people like to start their day right. The energized waking up keeps you active all day long. That's why we are trying to eat the right food types that will keep us safe, and always on the go. There are other ways to get the much-needed kick off the muscle. Some people prefer to drink energy drinks to provide them with that dose of vigour. Drinking energy drinks, however, has some negative effects on our overall health which is why many people are searching for a more natural way to get an energy boost. A 'good old coffee drink' is one of the more natural, and healthier beverages you can drink to keep you vigorous.

Get the coffee grounds, place them on your coffee maker and let them brew! Sure, a hot cup of coffee to kick off your day. It's Brewed Tea! Yeah, while we're talking about brewing a cup of coffee, are there any other ways you can prepare your coffee? Do you use other coffee devices, or only using the electric coffee maker that is always reliable? Would you want a mild flavour of coffee or a stronger and bolder flavour of coffee? We all have our tastes, but our passion for coffee is what binds us.

That there is an iconic coffee maker used by people since time immemorial? Yeah, up to the present, various families still use this coffee-maker. Want to know what that's like? Let's turn off the excitement and head straight for it. This famous coffee maker, the Moka Pot, is nothing but.

THE MOKA POT

What is Plant Moka?

The Moka Pot is the 'caffettiera,' or as the Italians call it. Moka Pot is a coffee maker that has been in the Italian household since the 1950s. This coffee-maker was invented and purchased by Luigi De Ponti, and patented by Alfonso Bialetti. This coffee maker brings a rich Italian culture you'll see a Moka Pot in nearly all Italian houses, according to some coffee enthusiasts. Without this iconic piece of homeware, an Italian kitchen won't be complete. This eighty-year-old coffee pot was used in various countries. It is mainly popular in European countries and has become a household name for Italy, Portugal and Spain.

Design

Alfonso Bialetti has given the Moka Pot its aluminium look, and the explanation for that is easy. Alfonso Bialetti 's company was in the French metalworking and aluminium market. During that time, the concept of using aluminium as the coffee-maker 's primary metal was considered an innovation. Aluminium was not known to be the primary metal that you are using for cooking products. In the limelight, the Moka Pot brought aluminium. At that time, several people had been suspicious about the Moka Pot due to certain health hazards. Because the pot was made of aluminium, it heats up quickly making handling difficult for people.

Concerning its success, the Moka Pot did not diminish. With the emergence of new products in the industry, the original design is still what most consumers are looking for. The Moka Pot is already on the market, right now. You can purchase the latest designs made, or you can still have the option to buy the original design.

There are no established Moka Pot manufacturers but the Bialetti company. Whether you think it's difficult to find this famous piece of kitchenware, don't worry, as there are online retailers offering both international purchases and Moka Pot delivery. This is a true testament to the fact that the Moka Pot is not just a coffee maker but a valuable piece in the coffee sector. It's going to be a piece of historical item that you can share with the next generation.

HOW DOES THIS POT WORK?

The Moka pot's coffee-brewing mechanism is very simple; you don't need to be a rocket scientist to understand how it works. It uses pressure to force hot water through the coffee on the table, how easy that is! The concept is innovative because the form works together with the other components or parts to produce dense and solid coffee. If the other part is missing, it won't yield great tasting coffee. So it's a unique design. If you are looking at our electric coffee makers, the design of these coffee makers has been based on the Moka Pot design.

It has a place where you put the ground of the coffee, a place where you put the water and an area where the coffee is made.

THREE MAIN PARTS OF THE MOKA POT.

Moka Pot has three main pieces; we have the bottom portion or called the bottom chamber where the water is put. You that the coffee grounds on the tube and container, and then the top chamber is where the steam or coffee is placed. Take note of the last paragraph; see how I moved the word and not drip it down. The new coffee makers are making use of the technique to drip coffee. Via a tube, the boiling water is directed to the coffee beans, as the coffee beans get the hot water, the coffee then drips to the cup. Take notice that hot water moves through the coffee grounds and not through the steam.

Because of the hot water, the Moka Pot uses steam, making the final product smoother and savoury. The Moka Pot uses a push effect or pushing the steam to move the ground coffee through. A Moka Pot produces a better-tasting coffee that is similar to espresso, according to coffee enthusiasts. This is why many people have become an enormous fan of the Moka Pot Express. The culture and tradition you obtain from using the Moka Pot is the primary reason why it is still the most sought-after piece of coffee equipment in the world and nowadays.

In the speciality coffee world, Moka pots have a bit of a bad name. It's a credibility won, but it's also false.

Historically Moka pot coffee has been very bitter, placing it at odds with speciality coffee goals. We are, however finding new and improved ways to brew this coffee style, and we are beginning to enjoy it again.

If you're just starting to learn about Moka pots or you're a seasoned veteran, this Moka Pot Coffee Ultimate Guide will be packed full of useful details from a coffee speciality perspective.

My mission is to inspire you to brew the best possible Moka pot coffee so if that sounds good to you, let's jump in!

WHAT A POT MOKA?

The Moka Pot is a stovetop coffee maker, produced in 1933 for Alfonso Bialetti by the inventor Luigi De Ponti. This new, art deco coffee maker has been adopted very fast throughout Italy.

People loved its ability to carry commercial espresso-like coffee to the average home (you must note that during this period, espresso was weaker).

The Moka Pot could be found in Europe by the late 1950s, and North America, North Africa, and the Near East were all starting to note the brewer.

Now, there are hundreds of Moka Pot companies and this brewer's many styles but Bialetti, the original Moka pot company, is still big. One of their best-sellers is their first and popular Bialetti Express.

Let's walk through the simple Moka pot building:

The body of stainless steel or aluminium is engineered to withstand heat from hot furnaces and to avoid damaging rust. A water chamber at the device's bottom holds the water while it is being heated.

A coffee basket is directly above the water chamber. This basket holds the grounds and features tiny holes at the bottom, allowing steam to rise from the coffee grounds and extract things (like oils, acids, flavours).

The filter screen is directly above the bowl, allowing the brewed coffee to rise (but not the grounds), through pressure, through a funnel, through a spout, and into the upper chamber.

Performance of Brewing explained

Since the water is heated in a (mostly) sealed setting, it causes a lot of pressure. This pressure releases water vapour to the table, which initiates the brewing process.

And this is not stopping there. The pressure in the funnel also pushes the liquid coffee up. This is no longer pressurized as it spills out into the upper chamber, but it comfortably fills the room.

The Misunderstanding of Stovetop Espresso

While being known as "stovetop espresso makers," it is not true that Moka pots do make espresso.

Espresso is produced at incredible 8-10 bars of pressure as hot water is pushed through fine coffee grounds. Only real espresso machines can create intense pressure.

The Moka pot usually produces a pressure of 1-2 inches. That is more than manually produced by humans, but nowhere near a true espresso machine.

So while the coffee is still quite concentrated, it is not exactly espresso. It's not passing the crema test (not enough pressure to form very fine cream).

Even, it's pretty similar to flavour-wise. Possibly, many people wouldn't know it's not espresso, so you can still use it to make drinks like espresso.

Top for a cappuccino or latte with steamed milk or an americano blend with hot chocolate. And if it's not genuine at 100 per cent, who cares if you like how it tastes?

STRENGTHS AND WEAKNESSES OF MOKA POT COFFEE

Moka pots are relatively easy to use and brew a rich and strong coffee that looks like an espresso. The design in aluminium or inoxidable steel is sturdy, durable and easy to clean.

They all come with a safety release valve that releases if too much pressure builds up, and can be easily used on most furnaces. Construction is also relatively simple, making them affordable.

There are a couple of drawbacks to remember though. They can be a little finicky at first and hard to find out. However, if you are not very cautious, the coffee will quickly turn very bitter.

LET 'S FIND IF THIS IS THE BREWER FOR you

Would you like to make espresso-like coffee affordably? Then get a Moka pot and save several hundred dollars by not buying a big espresso machine.

Wanna brew real espresso? Looking for more expensive espresso machines. However, there is no shame in going the less expensive route with a pot of Moka.

Will you enjoy thick, strong coffee that can be used in several different ways? Fantastic! Go ahead and have a Moka bowl to yourself.

Do you want a brewer with the no-learning curve? Yeah, hey. This one isn't crazy hard, but learning takes a bit of time. Perhaps the fastest way to get espresso-like coffee is, but the learning curve is there.

If you think the Moka Pot suits you best, let 's move on to some pre-brewing considerations.

THOUGHTS AND PRE-STEPS

A no-brainer, Fresh Coffee. Coffee beans can have fascinating and rich flavours that blow minds when at peak freshness-like blueberries, pine, or cane sugar.

Sadly, after just two weeks of roasting, those flavours decay. Ground coffee has just 30 minutes to go-sad!

Purchase freshly ground coffee and just grind it for moments before brewing. There is no other way of preserving your beans' fresh flavours.

Choose a Moka pot of the correct size. They 're sized to produce about one shot (1-2 ounces of intense coffee) in a 1-cup pot, two shots in a 2-cup, and so on.

Keep in mind: you can't half-fill a Moka bowl, so don't buy a 6-cup consider that now and then you can only make 3-cups full. They only work well when properly filled.

You are using a clear grind size from fine to medium-fine. You shouldn't go all out, using fine grinds of espresso. Those could block the filter screen and create a dangerous amount of pressure. Go for coffee which is just a bit finer than your average coffee grounds.

COFFEE POT MOKA GUIDE

Mind that everything here is consistency. Inconsistent grounds will brew unbalanced coffee-and you're going to feel sad for the best results using just a burr coffee grinder (skip past the blade grinders).

You are using delicious water which has not a very high content of calcium. Your coffee is 99.9 per cent water, and if you don't like your water's taste, you won't like your coffee's taste.

Pre-heat the water to that the time it takes for the Moka pot to sit on the burner. This also reduces the risk of the grounds being accidentally "cooked" while the pot warms up, which would damage the flavour and cause a lot of bitterness.

What about the Scale of Coffee? Normally I suggest weighing your coffee and water using a gram scale. That's not as important in this scenario.

You want the coffee basket to be loaded with grounds and to level it off with a knife. Then you want the water chamber filled to the bottom of the release valve. It's a pretty straightforward measuring process, so you don't even need a scale to match Moka Pots.

Although, theoretically, bean mass can vary between bean bags, so if you really want to be precise (or just grind the exact amount of beans you need), go ahead and use a coffee bean scale.

Now that you have considered these issues let's turn to the actual brewing (AKA, the fun part).

A Step-by-step Guide for MOKA POT COFFEE

Gather your ingredients and tools before you start.

- Freshly roasted coffee
- Hot Water
- Moka pot
- Cold towel
- Burr Grinder Coffee

We'll brew with a 2-Cup Moka Pot for this guide.

1. Grind enough coffee to fill the basket with coffee cup at a fine to the medium-fine setting. Take a knife with it, and level the field. Do not tamp down on the grounds.
2. Fill the water chamber up to the very bottom of the release valve with boiling water. Do not cover the valve, or if there is a pressure emergency, it will not work.
3. Go ahead and throw in the freezer, a damp kitchen towel.
4. Assemble the Moka Pot, making sure the ridges where the pieces screw together are no

grounds. Rogue grounds that are stuck here will prevent a full seal damaging the flavour and balance.
5. Place on the stove and turn medium-low heat on. To avoid getting too hot a handle, place it on the edge of the burner, if you can.
6. Relax and start a timer. It might take about 5-10 minutes before anything happens. If after 10 minutes nothing happens, turn the heat slightly upwards.
7. Coffee should eventually begin oozing up into the upper chamber. This means that the energy works, and the coffee brews. The heat is too strong if it's spurting and spewing-turn the baby down!
8. When the coffee is around 80 per cent up to the spout (or looks like golden honey), take it off the burner and immediately place it on the cold towel. Rapidly cooling the pot helps to prevent the bitter liquid added to the coffee from funnelling.
9. Pour in and serve right away. Enjoy it!

Chapter 8: ESPRESSO

THE HISTORY
In Europe during the 19th century, coffee was big business. The espresso was born as inventors tried to boost brews and the brewing time

Espresso is coffee, for many coffee drinkers. It is the purest coffee bean distillation, the absolute meaning of a bean. It's probably the first instant coffee, in a different way. It could take up to five minutes before espresso-five minutes! – For brewing a cup of coffee. Yet what exactly is espresso, and how did our daily rituals come to dominate?

While many people are familiar with espresso these days due to the world's Starbucksification, there is still some confusion about what it is – largely because of the "espresso roasts" available everywhere on supermarket shelves. First and most importantly, the espresso is not a method of roasting. It is not a bean, but a combination. It is a planning process. More specifically, it is a preparation process in which highly pressurized hot water is forced to create a very concentrated coffee drink with a rich, robust flavour over coffee grounds.

Although there is no systematic method for pulling an espresso shot, the concept of authentic espresso by Italian coffee maker Illy seems to be as good an indicator as any other:

A hot water jet at 88 °-93 °

C (190 ° -200 ° F) passed through a seven-gram (.25 oz) cake-like layer of ground and tamped coffee at a pressure of nine or more atmospheres. Done right, the effect is a concentration of pure sensory pleasure not exceeding 30 ml (one oz)

To those of you who, like me, are out of the science curriculum for more than a few years, nine pressure atmospheres are the equivalent of nine times the amount of pressure usually exerted by the earth's atmosphere. As you could tell from the accuracy of Illy's explanation, good espresso is good chemistry.

It is about precision and accuracy and finding the perfect balance between grinding, temperature, and pressure. Espresso exists molecularly. That's why technology was such an important part of espresso's historical growth and a key to the ongoing quest for the perfect shot. The devices – or Macchina – that make our cappuccinos and lattes have a history that stretches back more than a century, even though espresso was never built per se.

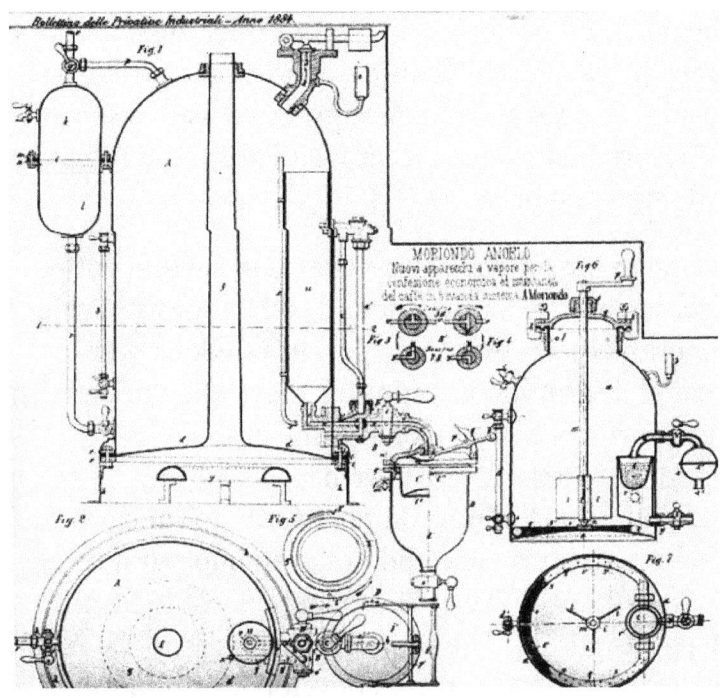

Coffee became a major industry in Europe in the 19th century, with cafes thriving throughout the mainland. Yet coffee brewing proceeded slow, and the customers often had to wait for their brew, as is still the case today. Seeing an opportunity, inventors throughout Europe started to investigate ways of reducing brewing time using steam engines – this was, after all, the age of steam. While there were countless patents and experiments, the invention of the machine and the process that would lead to espresso is usually credited to Angelo Moriondo of Turin, Italy, who in 1884 was awarded a patent for "modern steam machinery for economic and instant coffee beverage preparation."

The machine consisted of a large boiler, heated to 1.5 bar of pressure, which on-demand pushed water through a large bed of coffee grounds, with a second boiler producing steam that would flash the coffee bed and finish the brew.

Although Moriondo's invention was the first coffee machine to use both water and steam, for the Turin General Exposition, it was purely a bulk brewer created. Moriondo is not much more known, owing in large part to what we would think of today as a branding failure. There have never been any "Moriondo" machines; there are still no valid machines in existence and not even photographs of his work. Moriondo has been largely lost to history, except its patent. The same error should not be made by the two men who would develop Morinodo's design to create a single serving espresso.

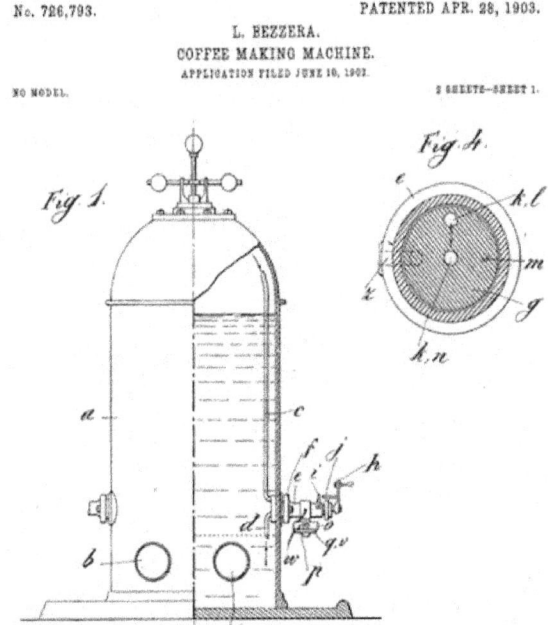

Luigi Bezerra and Desiderio Pavoni had been espresso's Steve Wozniak and Steve Jobs. Milanese fabricator and liquor manufacturer Luigi Bezzera had the know-how. In the early years of the 1900s, the patented single-shot espresso when finding a process for quickly brewing coffee directly into the cup. He made several improvements to the machine of Moriondo, introduced the portafilter, multiple brew heads and many other innovations that are still associated with today's espresso machines. In Bezzera 's original patent, a large boiler filled with water was heated up with built-in burner chambers until it pushed water and steam through a tamped ground coffee puck.

The system the heated water moved through also functioned as heat radiators, reducing the water temperature in the boiler from 250 ° F to an ideal brewing temperature of around 195 ° F (90 ° C). And voila, and espresso. A cup of coffee has been prepared to order for the first time in a matter of seconds. Yet Bezzera's computer was heated over an open flame, making it hard to regulate pressure and temperature, and almost impossible to make a clear shot. And quality is essential to the espresso environment.

Although there is no systematic method for pulling an espresso shot, the concept of authentic espresso by Italian coffee maker Illy seems to be as good an indicator as any other:

In 1903 Pavoni bought patents from Bezerra and improved several aspects of the design. Notably, he invented the first valve for removing strain. It ensured that from the quick release of pressure, hot coffee would not spill all over the barista, helping speed up the brewing cycle and anywhere receive the gratitude of baristas. Also, Pavoni invented the steam wand to control the built-up steam that was gathering within a boiler engine. Bezzera and Pavoni worked together to perfect their machine that was dubbed the Ideale by Pavoni. The two men introduced the world to 'cafeé espresso' at the 1906 Milan Fair.

While Bezzera might have even designed Pavoni's first machines, he gradually faded from the picture – he may have been bought out – as Pavoni proceeded to market his brand name "espresso" ("made on the spur of the moment") machines, which were commercially manufactured in his Milan workshop. The Ideale has marked an important phase in the first generation of modern espresso, with its various inventions.

Different espresso machines started to appear in Italy after the Milan Fair, and Bezzera 's early utilitarian machine developed into intricate golded contraptions that looked like a hood ornament for an airship in a novel by Jules Verne.

Such early machines could generate up to 1,000 cups of coffee an hour but rely solely on steam, that had the unfortunate effect of imbuing the coffee with a bitter or burnt but could only evoke, at best, two bars of atmospheric pressure – not even enough for the resulting drink to be known as espresso by today's standards. As electricity replaced gas and Art Deco replaced the early 20th-century chrome-and-brass aesthetics, the machines became smaller and more powerful. Still, no coffee innovators succeeded in producing a machine that could brew more than 1.5-2 bars of pressure without burning the coffee.

Over more than a decade, Pavoni dominated the espresso market. And amid his machinery's growth, espresso remained a largely regional delight for Milanese residents and nearby areas.

Pier Teresio Arduino was amongst Pavoni's rising competition. Arduino was an entrepreneur who was eager to find a method of brewing espresso that was not solely steam dependent. While he planned to integrate screw pistons and air pumps into the machines, he was never in a position to execute his ideas effectively. His key contributions to espresso's history are of a different type, instead. Arduino was a master marketer and businessman-more so than just Pavoni. He created a marketing machine around espresso, which included directing the graphic designer Leonetto Cappiello to produce the iconic espresso poster that depicted perfectly the essence of espresso and the pace of modern times.

Arduino had a much larger workshop in the 1920s than Pavoni's in Milan and was largely responsible for exporting machines from Milan and spreading the espresso across the rest of Europe as a result of his production capabilities and marketing skills.

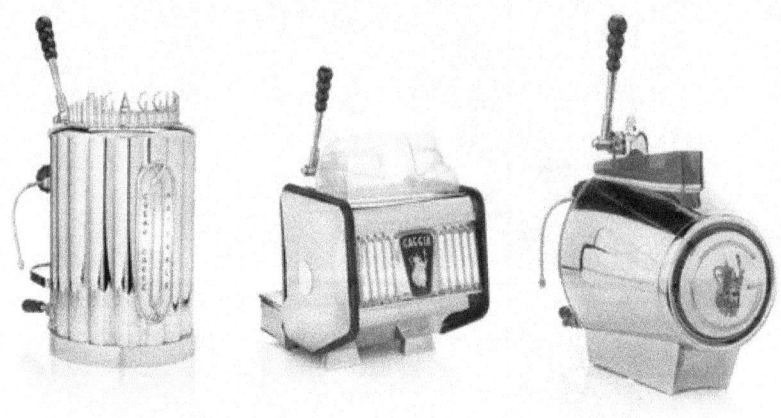

Milanese café owner Achille Gaggia was the man to eventually break the two bar brewing barrier. With the invention of the lever-driven machine, Gaggia turned the Jules Verne hood ornament into a chromed-out counter-top starship. In Gaggia's unit, which was developed after World War II, steam pressure in the boiler pushes the water into a cylinder where a spring-piston lever powered by the barista further pressures it. This not only eliminated the need for large boilers, but it also raised the water pressure from 1.5-2 bars to 8-10 bars. The lever machines even uniformed the espresso scale.

On lever groups the cylinder could accommodate just one ounce of water, reducing the amount that could be used to make an espresso. There also came some new jargon with the lever machines: baristas operating Gaggia's spring-loaded levers coined the term espresso "pulling a shot." But perhaps most significantly, the discovery of crema came with the invention of the high-pressure lever system – the foam floating over the coffee liquid, which is the defining characteristic of a quality espresso.

A historical anecdote suggests that early customers were wary of this "scum" floating over their coffee before Gaggia started referring to it as "Caffe cream," implying that the coffee was of such quality as to create its cream. Gaggia's lever unit, with high pressure and golden crema, marks the birth of contemporary espresso.

The espresso unit at Faema E61

But this is not, by far, the end of the Macchina's evolution though. The next revolution happens in the espresso machine, appropriately in the radical 1960s when the Faema E61 surpassed Gaggia's piston machine. Invented in 1961 by Ernesto Valente, the E61 launched several more developments and firsts of the espresso.

Rather than relying on the barista's manual force, it used a motorized pump to provide the nine atmospheric pressure bars needed for the espresso brewing.

The pump draws tap water immediately from a plumbing line and sends it through a spiral copper pipe inside a boiler before being fired through the ground coffee. A heat exchanger holds the water at an optimal temperature for brewing. The E61 was an instant success with its technological advances, smaller scale, flexibility and sleek stainless steel construction, and is rightly placed in the pantheon of the most popular coffee machines of history.

There are certainly a few more steps along the way, but those developments are tracking the espresso's larger commercial history. The espresso machine was greatly improved for more than a century, with electrical parts, computerized measurements and portable pneumatics. But as with the finest design objects, there isn't enough science and technology. There's always an element to the espresso. The barista's talent is just as critical as the consistency of the beans and machine output.

A successful espresso is said to be based on the four M's: Macchina, the espresso machine; Macinazione, a bean's proper grinding – a uniform grinding between fine and powdery – which is ideally done at moments brewing the drink; Miscela, the coffee blend and the roast, and Mano is the barista's skilled hand because even with the finest beans and the most advanced equipment, the shot is repeated Such four Ms, when properly combined, produce a drink that is bold and elegant at once, with a thin, sweet crema of foam floating over the coffee. A complex cocktail with a complicated track record.

10 FAMOUS DRINKS TO MAKE YOUR ESPRESSO MACHINE

1. Espresso

Okay, this one may seem a little repetitive, but knowing what espresso is should help you understand its place on this list in the rest of the drinks. Espresso is a highly concentrated, high-pressure coffee shot that is made. An espresso is usually 1.5 to 2 oz in volume using 18 g of coffee, with a standard double shot, depending on the barista or the store. The signature crema on top is the product of supersaturated coffee with CO_2 released during extraction which forms a layer of foam on top of it.

2. Cappuccino

Cappuccinos are balanced drinks typically consisting of 2 oz of espresso, vaporized milk and milk foam each. Served in a cappuccino cup, these drinks are great in addition to steamed milk, for those who love a bit of airy foam. If you are a foam addict, ask for a dry cappuccino, it substitutes all of the vaporized milk for milk foam. Consumers in the U.S. consume cappuccinos during the day, while in Italy, this is usually used as a breakfast treat.

3. Macchiato

There are two types of macchiatos actually, but we are condensing them into one single entry. The better-known espresso macchiato is an espresso shot, with a milk foam dollop. The espresso macchiato, translated from Italian as "dirty" or "spotted," is a great dessert drink for those who want a bit of caffeine but not a lot of liquid. The milk's richness is a major complement to the expresso's strong coffee flavour with the foam providing a touch of decadence. The latte macchiato, its much more popular latte equivalent, involves steaming equal parts of milk and milk foam and then adding a shot of espresso for a perfectly layered drink.

4. Américano

Invented during WWII for American soldiers stationed in Europe, the Americano was an attempt to emulate American coffee with espresso. Only add hot water from your espresso machine to the espresso you only made, easy peasy, to make it more. You can modify the amount of water used to make it as bold or as delicate as you want. You can also reverse the script by brewing espresso over hot water and making a drink known as Long Black.

5. latte

Lattes are one of the most popular, period, coffee beverages. The perfect latte, complete with latte art, is a foundational piece of coffee knowledge of any barista, consisting primarily of espresso and steamed milk, with just a touch of foam. A that take blends 2 oz of espresso served in a latte cup, with 10 oz of steamed milk.

6. Ristretto

A ristretto is an even more powerful and potent espresso shot. It uses the same amount of coffee, but is finer ground, and uses about half the amount of liquid. As the shot is pulled quicker, a ristretto 's balance would be different from an espresso, which involves a higher volume of quick extraction components.

7. Flat white

A flat white is more or less a latte made in cappuccino, mixing 2 oz of espresso with 4 oz of steamed milk. The flat means no foam whatsoever, implying it's just steamed milk like a latte but with much less pressure overall for a more forward coffee taste. While the debate rages over its exact origin, it is assumed that the flat white has made its first appearance in either New Zealand or Australia.

8. cortado

A cortado is an espresso beverage which is espresso and steamed milk in equal parts. Unlike a flat white part of espresso, two parts of milk, a cortado is 1/3 less liquid, which means it is served in a smaller cup and is a smaller overall drink. It's the perfect drink for someone who loves a latte's taste and mouthfeel but needs a little more coffee taste and substantially less liquid.

9. Tonic and Espresso

A popular summer drink combining coffee science with cocktail science, Espresso and Tonic is a refreshing take on the Gin and Tonic classics. You are using a vivid, fruity coffee such as a natural Kenya AA or an Ethiopia for better results. The interplay with the bubbly, bittersweet tonic with fruity and acidic flavours is fantastic. If you feel fancy, add a squeeze of lime, and lime to garnish.

10. Affogato

An affogato is a dessert beverage which combines an espresso shot with a vanilla ice cream scoop. Hot and cold, vivid and smooth, the contrast between the espresso and the ice cream maker for a tasty treat that you can add to your menu.

MISUNDERSTANDINGS ON ESPRESSO

Let's move on to some misconceptions about espresso.

Maybe the biggest: Bitter is the espresso.

That possibly was back when espresso was made with steam. The high steam temperature over-extracted the coffee, creating bitter flavours, and the coffee's consistency probably didn't help much. But it is a different story today. For some cases, espresso is a bitter cocktail. Healthy and sometimes chocolaty, the high-quality Italian-style blends of today. There is a whole new world of options such as single-origin and high-altitude coffees with notes of fruit, floral and berry, so there are plenty of options to choose from to avoid any bitter coffee.

First is the belief that caffeine packs espresso.

A shot of espresso contains 30 to 50 milligrams, according to the National Coffee Association. Compared to an 8-ounce standard coffee cup which has between 65 and 120 milligrams. So the caffeine in the espresso is more concentrated, but there's typically more caffeine in a cup of drip coffee at standard serving sizes.

Our final misconception is that an espresso is a form of coffee or a variety of beans.

To clear this up, you'll see espresso on some beans' labels, particularly on bean blends, but espresso is a method of brewing and not a specific form of coffee.

We should not, therefore, be permitted to make espresso from any coffee bean. Indeed, the trend in recent years has been more exotic varieties as the world of espresso drinking moves away from traditional dark roasted bean blends and into medium roast coffees with distinct flavours, as is the case with single-origin beans, shade-grown, and high-altitude coffees that grow slower and concentrate more flavour in the bean.

A COMPLETE LIST OF COFFEE DRINKS OF EVERY TYPE

A quick visit to the coffee shop will tell you what you need to know about how many coffee varieties there are-even if you tried, you couldn't count them what.

There are so many different brews, beans, and styles that in one lifetime you probably won't be able to taste these. But that's not to suggest you shouldn't try.

In this guide, we'll look at the three most widely consumed types of coffee drinks and a wide variety of their subtypes.

Black Coffee

Simply put, black coffee is a mixture without any milk, of water and coffee. It should be eaten with no added flavours like sugar, cream and milk. Adding those things improves the coffee's scent and colour, rendering it lighter-brown or white.

This may seem easy, but you should know that there are different ways to serve this coffee, and each of them has different influences on the taste. Let's look more closely at the most notable types of black coffee.

Espresso

The Espresso is a popular Italian form of coffee. You make this by forcing steam from high pressure through grounded coffee beans. The final product is a thick, creamy foamed coffee on top. It is often a base for other coffee drinks such as Americano, due to its thickness and high level of caffeine per unit.

Espresso is one of Italy's most popular coffees which serves as a basis for most other types of coffee.

Ristretto

Ristretto, short in Italian, is an espresso shot made like standard espresso but with half the sugar. So the result is a more concentrated espresso shot with a slightly different flavour.

Américano

A caffè americano is an American coffee term in Italian. The name is believed to come from the U.S.

soldiers in Italy during World War II, who used water to ration the scarce quantities of espresso available at the time.

The Americano foundation is espresso. To make the espresso weaker, a larger amount of hot water is poured over it, turning a small shot of espresso into a big cup of coffee.

Long Black

Long black has a better taste compared to American. You do it by pouring two ristretto or espresso shots over a smaller volume of beer, thus improving the flavour.

Doppio

Doppio is a double espresso shot or Double in English. With a double sputter, it goes through the portafilter. Doppio is also considered the default espresso shot these days.

Pour over-coffee

Pouring over coffee is a technique that refreshes the water that surrounds the grounded coffee. A bottle, a 'pour-over dripper' and freshly ground coffee are included. The cycle is composed of three stages, each adding to the distinctive consistency and taste of the coffee. That involves humidifying, dissolving, and diffusion. Read our guide to beginners for a coffee over here.

Drip coffee

Drip coffee, as the name implies, means dripping cup boiling water over ground coffee. The water goes through the filter, into the bowl. This is a slower process than standard espresso making. In the end, though, you'll get a better coffee.

Batch brew

The most recent way to serve dark coffee is by the Batch brew process. Instead of old-timer filter coffee machines, modern technology enables cafés to make filter coffee of higher quality cheaply and easily.

Matt Perger, a twice-time Australian Barista champion, explained why (1) his coffee shop in Melbourne had batch brew introduced.

Instant Coffee

Instant coffee is one of the easiest for producing coffees. You simply pour over the coffee powder or crystals the desired amount of hot water and swirl until it dissolves. Instant coffee isn't that great, but special drinks such as Dalgona Coffee can be made with this.

It has a shelf-life much longer than most other coffees and differs in popularity across the world. In Britain, for example, it still accounts for more than 70 per cent of all coffee purchased. At the other hand, it is routinely bought by only 7 per cent of Americans and a mere 1 per cent of the French (2).

Here is where we have described the best instant coffee tasting brands we recommend and ever wondered how the coffee is made instantaneously? Ok, here's how.

AeroPress Coffeé

You need to use an AeroPress system to make that form of coffee. The process looks like this: you put a paper filter or metal filter inside the tube, steep the coffee for less than a minute and then press it with a plunger through the filter. This coffee has a distinctive taste, thanks to the filter that stops oil and sediment from entering the cup.

Vacuum Coffeé

The coffee vacuum pot, used for making this form of coffee, has a history that spans more than two centuries (3). The vacuum maker has a lower vessel and an upper one. In the lower vessel, water boils while the ground remains at the upper part. The vacuum and the heat pressure pushes up the water and brews the coffee. The liquid falls into the bottom vessel until the heating ends, and is ready for serving.

Immersion Coffee

Immersion coffee is made by dipping the beans into boiling water where they have been steep for a while to improve the flavour. French press coffee is one of immersion coffee's most common variants. It is made from coarsely ground beans that are soaked for no more than five minutes in near-boiling water.

Milk-based coffee

With many people opting for one of the black varieties, adding milk to your coffee will give you a special kind of flavour. Other than that, because of the use of foamed milk, baristas enjoy milk-based coffee which allows them to decorate their coffee in stunning ways.

Milk-based coffee also contains lower levels of caffeine and acidity, making the coffee the best for the evening hours (4). As with black, milk-based coffee also includes many different coffee types.

White Flat

Flat white is a popular coffee based on milk that consists of espresso with a smaller amount of steamed milk. The scent is still dominated by the espresso taste, while the milk acts as a soothing flavour. But it's not the same as a white coffee (which is a Yemen-born coffee bean).

Cappuccino

Often, cappuccino is made from espresso and milk. There are two kinds of milk here, though. The coffee contains 1/3 of espresso, 1/3 of foamed milk and 1/3 of vaporized milk. Instead of milk, you can drink it iced, dry, with cream and in many other ways.

Latte

A Caffè latte is different from cappuccino because it contains a lot of milk, whereas cappuccino retains the stronger taste of espresso. A Latte, however, is not the same as a flat white, which is a common misconception. Flat whites have far fewer milk/bubbles that are foamed.

Out of all milk-based coffees a Latte usually has the 'milkiest' aroma.

Caffe breve

Caffè breve, which means short in Italian, is an American version of a latte consisting of 1/4 of espresso, 1/2 of vaporized milk and 1/2 of milk foam.

Because of the steamed half-and-a-half milk, which increases the volume of the foam, it is a bit thicker than the regular latte. It's considered so rich that typically there's no need to add sugar or some other sweetener. It is served mostly as a dessert beverage.

Piccolo Latte

Piccolo latte, or a little latte, is made by pouring warm milk over a shot of ristretto. Usually, cafés serve it in a small 100ml latte bottle, so it's essentially a little coffee shot with milk.

Other names for this coffee include Cataldo (Spanish) and Mezzo-Mezzo (Australian) for example.

Since it can be overwhelming to drink two or three full-sized milk coffees a day, drinking a few of those smaller caffeinated milk shots can be a perfect replacement.

Macchiato

A Macchiato is a strong coffee shot, with only a little milk. It is fair to say that the common definition of a macchiato is an espresso shot with a small splash of milk, originally from Italy (and translating to stain or mark). But you can get something slightly different, depending on where you are in the world and what cup you are using.

Macchiato Latte

Latte macchiato means "stained milk," and by pouring espresso over it, this beverage is simply a glass of milk that you "stain."

It is made and served differently but has the same ingredients as caffè latte. A great latte macchiato comes in a tall bowl, and the layers of foam on top, espresso in the centre, and milk at the bottom are visible.

Cortado

Cortado is a good mix of espresso and steamed milk, with a smooth texture similar to a frothy latte, cappuccino and the likes.

It doesn't have as much foam, and the coffee/milk ratio can be 1:1 to 1:2. It is usually served in a special glass with a handle and base made of metal wire. The glass will have a capacity between 150-200ml.

It is very popular in Spain, Portugal and Latin America. Here's how you could create your own.

Gibraltar

Cortado coffee is the most common variety in Gibraltar. It is a San Francisco cult coffee served in the popular 'Gibraltar' glasses. It is slightly colder than a standard Cortado with a richer texture.

Standard Gibraltar is made by adding an 85ml of milk and an espresso shot to a heated 'Gibraltar' bottle. The biggest drawback with Gibraltar, however, is that the glass can't hold up the heat, so the coffee cools very easily. You should then drink it fast for the optimum experience.

Moka(Casino)

The Mochaccino is a variety of café latte (not the same, as surprisingly many people believe). It consists of a double shot of espresso, foamed milk and an extra flavour. The scent typically comes from cocoa powder or syrup from chocolate. You can add a few cinnamon, whipped cream or other toppings if you want.

The Moka is like a rich chocolate coffee-perfect for casual coffee drinks because it's typically a coffee gateway.

Iced And Hot Coffees

Iced coffee is a great blend between refreshing beverages and a calming scent of coffee. You can do it in two distinct ways. One way is to brew it cold, which gives it a different flavour, and the other is to make it hot and then cool it down with ice, cold milk, or even ice.

Coffee Cold Brew

You can quickly make the cold brew coffee. Just mix the ground coffee with the cold water, steer it and leave it overnight in the refrigerator. After that, strain the mixture to extract and drink the remaining coffee any way you want.

One of the main characteristics of cold brewing is its smaller amount of caffeine

Nitro Coffee

This is a unique cold-served coffee with a creamy, beer-like feel, particularly as it is typically served in a beer bar. The thickness comes from nitrogen, which is impregnated with the coffee.

Iced Japanese Coffee

This coffee has a special way to make a brew. You brew it in hot water, then spill it over ice immediately. Ice contact will help release all the flavours which usually take hours to produce.

Tonic Espresso

You will brew two shots of espresso to make this refreshing drink, and leave them to cool. Later, you need to fill ice with a 0.2l (about 6.7 fl oz) glass, squeeze out some lime juice, then slowly pour the tonic water and the espresso shots together.

Strange And Unique Coffees

The coffees, as mentioned above, are most common but originate mainly from the United States and

Italian cuisines and cafés. There are diverse other cultures, however, that brew unique and distinctive aromas. Here are some of the world's strangest and most unique coffees.

Turkish Coffeé

You need finely ground coffee beans and a traditional Turkish pot called cezve to prepare a proper Turkish coffee. In the cezve heat the water and sugar until it boils, then place the ground coffee inside. You can reheat it quickly to get the perfect foam. It is unfiltered, meaning the remains of coffee powder end up in the cup, too.

Vietnamese Coffeé

Typically, Vietnamese coffee is dripped via a small Vietnamese metal filter. Sweetened milk can be used to serve it hot or cold.

Egg coffee is also a Vietnamese beverage, where egg yolks are pounded until they are smooth and then added along with condensed milk to the coffee and sugar. There is also a Swedish version of this beverage which is prepared in almost the same way but does not contain milk

Bulletproof Coffee

Bulletproof coffee is a combination of brewed coffee, coconut oil and unsalted butter. It is very popular with people on a high-fat, low-carb diet, and can serve as a breakfast substitute. This is not recommended, though, because your body does not receive all the essential nutrients that it needs for the day.

Butter coffee is identical to bulletproof coffee and consists of brewed coffee, unsalted butter and medium-chain triglycerides (MCTs). MCTs, which the human body easily digests, are readily available in stores in the form of oil that is added to the coffee.

Cascara Coffeé

What is Coffee Cascara? It's more of a regular coffee than a tea. You use coffee cherry leaves instead of producing it with coffee beans, which are excellent at alleviating digestive issues and constipation.

Kopi Luwak

Kopi Luwak probably isn't for everyone. It comes from Asian palm civet faeces, a small viverrid which eats coffee cherries. During digestion, the cherries ferment and then the farmers collect them from Kopi Luwak. It is considered an exotic coffee, at absurdly high prices.

Geisha Coffeé

Geisha coffee is a unique aroma and flavour, Ethiopian coffee. It is reportedly one of the world's most expensive coffees, attaining a price of $803 per pound in March 2019.

Affogato

Affogato is an Italian speciality consisting of a vanilla ice cream scoop in a glass with a hot espresso shot poured over it. There are also versions of the beverage that add an amaretto shot or some other alcoholic beverage.

Irish Coffeé

Irish coffee is a mixture of hot coffee, whisky and sugar. It is one of the world's most popular regular-coffee derivatives. In this walkthrough recipe, we'll show you how to make an authentic Irish coffee.

All these kinds of drinks are just the tip of the iceberg. Despite coffee being an integral part of cultures and history around the world, you will always find a new variety you have never encountered before. Hopefully, this article helped you discover some of your favourite drink's new varieties. But remember it's just a beginning.

Chapter 9: THE AMERICAN COFFEE

A History Of American Culture of Coffee

Coffee is as much an important part of American culture as blue jeans and rock-n-roll. The US has since revolutionized the coffee scene, from the launch of Starbucks to the recent revival of coffee traditions and skills, despite having a late start on the coffee wagon.

Like other foods, the origin of coffee is a convoluted tale within centuries-old mythology. A popular legend tells of a goat herder named Kaldi who, it is said, discovered coffee beans hundreds of years ago on the Ethiopian plateau. His goats, which snacked on the old fruit-bearing shrubs, galloped packed with the energy around him. Kaldi had a similar reaction, examining the fruit himself, sharing his finding with a nearby monastery. The abbot – who made a red berry beverage – shared the drink with other monks and distributed knowledge of the natural stimulant quickly across the continent.

Its cherry-like fruit was used in a variety of preparations before a modern version of coffee appeared, some of which included wine-like substances. By the fifteenth century, coffee was grown and traded in Arabia and roasted and brewed its beans – stripped from its pulp exterior. Public coffee houses, known as qahveh Khanh, sprung up eastward as places where people could share knowledge over a cup of the much-loved potion. Travelling to Europe, coffee soon became the favoured morning drink over beer and wine, and by the mid-1600s London had over 300 coffee houses – mostly frequented by prominent artists, authors, and intellects.

In the mid-17th century, the British eventually introduced coffee to the New World. Coffee houses were common, but it wasn't until 1773 when the Boston Party changed America's coffee culture forever: the revolt against King George III generated a mass switch among the colonists from tea to coffee. Coffee demand flourished, and coffee cultivation expanded outside of Arabia for the first time after the Dutch had secured coffee seedlings towards the end of the 1600s. Travellers and traders carried seeds to new lands and planted coffee trees all over the globe.

By the 18th century, coffee had become one of the most valuable commodities in the world. Consumption and popularity increased in the US, especially during the Civil War, and savvy entrepreneurs were looking for a way to benefit from it. In 1864 the brother's John and Charles Arbuckle, born in Pittsburgh, began selling pre-roasted coffee by the pound, becoming rich by selling it to cowboys in the West. James Folger, who has sold coffee to California's gold miners, has also seen great success. Several other big-name coffee brands, including Maxwell House and Hills Brothers, followed suit very quickly. Instant coffee was introduced to the market in the aftermath of the war and remained popular until Starbucks opened in 1971.

Starbucks locally made coffee available to customers across America, tailoring the beverage to each customer's particular palate.

Today the coffee revolution keeps on rising. A grassroots movement that started in small, independently owned coffee shops is transforming what Starbucks brought us: it is now an innovative craft – much like that of wine or beer – that uses fair-trade beans that are organic, locally roasted. Where the beans are grown, how they are roasted and where the brewing process is all closely looked at. This expertise in coffee grows among young people, many of whom use it as preparation for the culinary world.

Just like a string of fresh rosemary or juicy, ripe tomato carries a multitude of complex aromas, so makes coffee.

What Is Drip Coffee?

You may or may not be familiar with the word "drip coffee," enough to say; I do not doubt that if you've drunk coffee ever in your life, you've had a drip coffee. Simply put, drip coffee is coffee that the coffee makers are brewing. You may argue that anything like a French press or a percolator is also a coffee maker, but in this sense "drip coffee" refers to coffee produced by an automatic coffee maker, which means a carafe and a basket full of ground coffee with hot water dripped on it.

We mainly use the word drip as a way of separating coffee from espresso, as espresso is made from coffee and technically coffee itself. Right, that can get confusing. If you haven't already, check out our full guide.

So why is it known as drip coffee? Yeah, it all has to do with how you brew the coffee. The brewing method looks something like this at an automated coffee maker:

1. A filter is loaded into the coffee maker, full of ground coffee.
2. Water is filled to the reservoir.
3. A heating device heats the water and pushes it upward.
4. Water runs to ahead of the shower and is dripped onto the ground-filled coffee filter.
5. Brewed coffee flows out into a carafe and the basket.

What differentiates Drip Coffee?

Drip coffee relies on thermally induced pressure to send it to the showerhead compared to espresso, and gravity to drag it through the ground. It dissolves significantly less of the soluble mass of the coffee, and the paper filters common to this brewing method will trap many of the oils that otherwise would be present in espresso, French press, or percolator coffee. This way, brewing coffee is uncomplicated, inexpensive and therefore extremely popular among Americans to whom "drip coffee" is just "coffee."

The word "brewed coffee" is often used by the more barista inclined to refer to manual methods of coffee brewing such as pour-over. The words "custom coffee" or "artisan coffee" are somewhat interchangeable, and the general meaning is that the creativity and effort went into producing it. Drip coffee is the result of automated operation, placing the grinds in, pouring the water in and pressing the button. Maybe you're deciding how many cups you like, or you're setting the timer to your coffee maker, so it stops blinking at you "noon," but that's all about it.

Before we continue, I want to make it clear that the term "drip coffee" is not a disappointment, but merely a descriptor of what is perhaps America's most common brewing method, though one that requires considerably less effort than others.

Making Drip Coffee

Growing up, the answers to these questions was "1 scoop for every 2 cups," but I do not believe this is the answer you've found. A successful starting point is with a ratio of 60 g of dry coffee (beans or soil) to 1l of water. But let's do some maths and come up with some basic averages.

The typical American cup of coffee is 8 oz liquid, and 33.814 oz is 1 litre. Which means to be exact, you get just over four full cups for every litre (4.22675). If you do some rounding, that means you'll want around 14 g of coffee for every 8 oz cup of coffee, which is just about 0.5 oz. Our takeaway, then, is:

For every 8 oz cup of coffee, you want to brew, using about 14 g or 0.5 oz of dry coffee.

DRIP COFFEE vs POUR OVER

In the speciality world, Pour over coffee is a much-revered method of brewing coffee. In short, pouring over brewing means pouring hot water over ground coffee that drains into a carafe and through a filter.

Although that might sound like drip coffee, it is very different actually. As noted above, drip coffee is the product of automatically dripping water from a coffee maker. Your role is limited to making the raw materials available and to pressing click.

You're the one who pours over the water, regulates the flow, stirs your grinds and adjusts the filter. It is a fully manual process which needs constant involvement to get correct. In the drip coffee case, one of the main advantages of choosing drip is comfort, and at the end of the day when you've just woken up, that's a big deal.

Is Pour Over Coffee good?

Although it takes time to pour over, it can deliver some of the best coffee you can taste.

A very loaded question, but a valid one, is whether it is easier to pour-over coffee than to drip coffee. So let's get into it. The short answer is yes. Faced with it, it's pretty easy to see why to pour over as a process needs greater adherence to the speciality coffee brewing criteria to be successfully implemented. If you grind your beans fresh at the very least, and you have a digital kettle to heat your water to the correct brewing temperature, you are already pulling ahead of the drip.

Diving a little deeper, it is important to remember that, in addition to precise measures for the total amount of ground coffee and water used for brewing, best practices for pouring over brewing include strict regulation of water flow when pouring; certainly more reliable than measuring in scoops. Ultimately, regulating the water flow and using the correct grinding will provide you with the appropriate contact time between the water and the ground coffee, which will avoid over or under extraction.

The resulting cup of coffee from a well-executed pour-over can yield far greater complexity of flavour, which ultimately results from greater control of the variable.

DRIP vs AMERICANO

The Cafe Americano was born in the WWII era in Europe, where American GIs wanted a coffee that reminded them of what they used to return home. An Americano is a mixture of espresso and hot water which ultimately determines the ratio by the tastes of the drinker. What's important to remember is that the Americans who were initially intoxicated by our soldiers weren't exactly what you'd be seeing today.

The revolutionary changes made by Achille Gaggia to the espresso brewing process did not take place until 1947 when he introduced a piston lever design. Thus the espresso initially used in Americanos had distinctly different characteristics from those of a modern shot, such as the absence of the so far known signature crema. Because the American uses espresso as its main component of coffee, it inherits some characteristics of espresso, naturally. An Americano should usually be more full-bodied and richer in flavour than drip coffee. You may also be able to preserve a light layer of crema on top of your cup, depending on how aggressively you add the water.

If you flip upside-down Under that process, you can also make a Long Black as you enjoy in Australia where a shot of espresso is brewed over hot water, preserving even more cream.

The primary explanation for more full-bodied flavours offered by Americano is the higher amount of dissolved solids contained in espresso, as compared to the comparatively lower amount contained in drip coffee. That also means an American will, on average, contain less caffeine than a cup of drip coffee.

DRIP COFFEE vs FRENCH PRESS
The French press, another extremely common form of brewing coffee. This also varies in preparation and flavour from the drip. Anyone who has enjoyed French press coffee knows the coffee from a coffee maker is smoother and more full-bodied than normal. It is due to the lack of a paper coffee filter to capture the aromatic oils that are emulsified when brewing from the ground coffee.

Also, French presses make it easier to remove uniformly because all the grounds are immersed in water when brewing. You're usually going to grind your coffee, add it to your carafe, pour in your tea, give it a swirl to get it all evenly and you're good to go. If you're just getting started, check out our full guide to French presses for more tips.

Barley coffee: what it is, and how it should be made

What is coffee made from barley? This is a non-alcoholic drink made from the infusion of a very ancient cereal, barley, already roasted and grounded.

The origins of this product 's vast diffusion go back to its cheap content. This quality-made this drink particularly appealing during the Second World War when traditional coffee had almost become a luxury for most of the population.

Today barley coffee remains a firm favourite among customers not only because of its quality but also because of the many health benefits it has on the organism: let 's find out what it is.

Chapter 10: BARLEY COFFEE

The barley coffee is a traditional Italian drink, and we may describe it as a replacement for classic espresso, which is made with the previously toasted and finely ground barley infusion, in the abundance of boiling water and therefore does not contain caffeine. It can be prepared conventionally by using the same machines for the espresso or coffee (Moka), or by diluting the extract directly into granules or powder such as soluble barley, for example, directly in very hot water.

Single portions for use in Moka, with the inside of the filter made from fibrous material, or the specially built machines for making your home barley coffee can be found on the market. A barley coffee made from the same classic espresso machine is not aesthetically quite appealing in appearance, though making it as automatic for barley as a classic coffee machine with its unique machine, you can still have the enticing surface foam used in the espresso.

In Italy, there are many shops where you can easily buy the barley, either at the bar or in a restaurant, such as in coffee shops, supermarkets, or if you want to eat in your moments of relaxation and away from home, there are now automatic hot drink dispensers that carry a medium-quality product.

The barley was already known long before decaffeinated coffee was introduced, particularly among people who can not drink caffeine for physical reasons or those who do not like the taste of the classic coffee. Even children are particularly fond of this drink in combination with fresh milk, and its intake is often targeted at pregnant women or during breastfeeding, for those who pursue special heart disease medical treatments or simply for those suffering from anxiety-related disorders.

Nutritional Values

Coffee Moka with barley

The barley coffee, being a soft drink, does not provide a high-calorie level for consumption, in fact, only add 15 grams of this soluble powder for the preparation of a large cup of about 250 ml of boiling water. In this way, you will get a product with a calorie amount equal to 20 Kcal per 100 ml of product.

It is not easy to assess the degree of dissolution of the molecules present in the barley dust when combined water, so we will describe only the soluble product from the nutritional point of view. Many calories in this drink are extracted from complex carbohydrates, as opposed to the nearly non-existent proteins and fats. Also absent are fibres and cholesterol, but about vitamin presents, it had to be known that the soluble barley has an abundant concentration of phosphorus and potassium as well.

This drink, considered harmless and caffeine-free, is highly valued in the world. Still, we must not forget that any food that is produced with roasting, as in this case, produces a substance called "acrylamide" in very significant amounts, toxic to the body. We suggest consumption not more than twice a day, with a quantity of about 10 grams. A cup a day with the prescribed dose above causes no physical harm to the body.

Barley coffee consumption is open to all except those suffering from celiac disease, as barley is a gluten-containing cereal. Therefore, it is not recommended for daily or occasional use in people with this important problem. As regards dietary food schemes for both bodyweight management, both for problems related to obesity, barley coffee intake, does not cause complications, and also for those suffering from diseases linked to the incorrect metabolic functioning, with lactose intolerances and even for vegetarian, vegan or religious diets.

Diffusion

The barley coffee, and that extracted from chicory, became the only and most popular drink in Europe during World War II. Such foods were used in the absence of coffee, which was difficult to obtain at the time, in addition to having a very high cost. In Spain, the barley coffee drank in the long post-war era was considered the drink of the poor, or a cheap substitute for coffee, thus taking on a very negative image that is still present among the people. The dozens of barley manufacturers that were present in the Spanish territory until 1950 have closed their operations, and we can count only two to date.

However, in Italy, barley coffee is a very popular drink, and now there are hundreds of companies dealing with this product's development. This is because it was rediscovered as a healthy drink instead of espresso, which in many cases is not suggested due to the new disease of the modern era, especially heart problems due to the sedentary life of our days. Thanks to its good nature, the barley coffee knows new fame, and many Italians are now drinking it.

Barley Coffee Benefits

Like chicory coffee, barley coffee is caffeine-free and therefore provides an alternative to espresso that is "lightweight." Additionally, this beverage will give the organism various health benefits if consumed regularly:

- Stimulates digestive juices and encourages digestion.
- Decreases abdominal swelling.
- Relieves constipation and encourages the flow of food into the intestine.
- Helps to reduce blood sugar.
- The anti-inflammatory agent is effective.
- Barley coffee is generally a true mine of healthy nutrients, including phosphorous, magnesium, vitamin E, group B vitamins, and potassium.

How is barley coffee made?

Barley coffee can be cooked in different ways. Some of these are not commonly used, such as the process by which the traditional pot used for Turkish coffee is used. Instead, other approaches that are more common include using soluble barley, the espresso machine and the Moka coffee pot.

Soluble Garlic

One of the easiest, most practical alternatives is to use powdered barley coffee which can be dissolved instantly into hot water or milk. Soluble barley coffee can be found easily at all supermarkets.

Coffee barley in capsules or in pods

Those who choose to use capsules or pods to make it with an espresso machine will be familiar with this preparation method which proves just as quick and convenient when used to make this alternative to the usual espresso.

The process to be followed is extremely simple and intuitive: all you need to do is insert the capsule or barley pod into the machine, push the button and wait for the extraction of the beverage.

How to make Moka coffee with barley coffee

The classic technique used to prepare coffee with Moka pot can also be used to make coffee from barley:

1. Up to the valve fill the base of the Moka pot full of cold water.

2. Place the filter on the base and fill with a teaspoon of ground barley.

3. Screw on the top and bring the Moka pot at low heat onto the hob. The drink is ready to be poured into your favourite espresso cups, after a few minutes.

Healthy and also very low calorie, barley coffee is the perfect start to any day, even when you're out and about: here are a few tips on how to enjoy a healthy breakfast at the bar.

The production of coffee from barley extends 2,000 years. It was drunk by the Greeks and the Romans to benefit from its energizing, physical and mental properties. That healthy habit has survived to this day.

That is real. Barley coffee – which is called coffee since it does not contain coffee beans and is made by the simple infusion of ground roasted barley – is now considered to be the most classic coffee substitute. Alternative beverages to coffee have been at the heart of a true boom in recent years, and barley coffee was no exception. Find out why that simple rustic brew is so popular!

THE ATTRIBUTES OF BARLEY COFFEE

Barley coffee preserves all of the qualities and advantages of the plant it is made from:

Rich in starch

Starch is a carbohydrate easily assimilated by our bodies: it does not give us a typical boost in caffeine, but rather a gradual dose of energy and well-being.

Caffeine-free

Someone who has trouble with the stomach, anxiety or insomnia and wants to avoid caffeine should replace classic barley coffee.

Small quantities of silicon

It's easy to digest and doesn't prevent sleep: it's ideal at any time of day. Safe fat and calories free

It doesn't make you fat, and those with high cholesterol can also drink it.

Except for celiacs – barley is a gluten-containing grain – this infusion does not have contraindications and is recommended for everyone, including infants, elderly women and pregnant women. You are permitted to drink 3 to 5 cups a day. The undesirable effects of acrylamide, a molecule produced during the roasting process, could arise only in cases of prolonged and excessive consumption: the same results we would experience if we eat only fried and burnt food every day and months. Barley Coffee: How to make it at home

You will find Barley coffee in bottles, in jars and packets. Here's a simple way of doing it:

1. Using an espresso-maker in a conventional way
2. For a Moka pot, just fill the filter half full
3. Instant barley coffee dissolved in boiling water
4. By System of Infusion. Pour two barley coffee tablespoons into a half-litre of boiling water. Return the water to the boil, remove from heat and let the barley settle down. Then filter it over a strainer.

You can sweeten the barley coffee as you please with milk, honey or brown sugar ... but don't overdo it!

With its light aromatic taste, Barley coffee is ideal for those who love natural yet delicious flavours. An ideal alternative to coffee, it can be enjoyed at any time of the day.

Chapter 11: GINSENG IN COFFEE

Ginseng supports the body and mind in several ways. Its medicinal use dates back thousands of years, particularly in ancient China.

What exactly is Ginseng?

Ginseng is the root of a plant called Panax, a small perennial shrub whose name means "remedy for all" in ancient Greek, panacea in Italian. On the other hand, the word ginseng derives from the Chinese and means "the human plant" because of the form of the tubers that very much mimic the human body, with arms and legs. The ginseng plant's root is 2 to 3 inches long (though occasionally doubling the size) and 1/2 to 1 inch thick.

There are eleven varieties of ginseng, with the most important originating from Europe, China and Korea. Ginseng is often mixed with other ingredients, with its bitter taste in nature, making it easier to drink.

For hundreds of years, as well as a powerful aphrodisiac, the Chinese found this "miraculous" root to be an anti-ageing and energy-boosting elixir. Even it is chewed on its own in some rural regions. Ginseng has, however, also been cooked in soups, and combined with hot tea. Now, it's blended with premium coffee to enhance its intensity and spruce up the natural flavour of the ginseng.

What is Ginseng 's benefit?

It decreases stress and tiredness and increases memory, concentration and mood. Ginseng can enhance the processes of thought and cognition. Research published in The Cochrane Library looked at the consistency and integrity of this argument. Ginseng has demonstrated benefits for memory, actions, and quality of life, the study reports.

Also, as per the experimental results in the Journal of Translational Medicine, ginseng can have anti-inflammatory effects. This "miracle" route also helps to alleviate inflammation. The researchers related ginseng to targeting immune system mechanisms that could reduce inflammation.

Finally, men might be taking ginseng to treat erectile dysfunction. Korean research in 2002 found that about 60 per cent of men who took ginseng reported a change in their symptoms. Also, research carried out by the British Journal of Clinical Pharmacology further claimed to provide "evidence of red ginseng's efficacy in the treatment of erectile dysfunction."

Ginseng coffee is one of the most common alternatives to a classic espresso, which has become increasingly popular by the day and is consumed both at home and in the bar.

This version has a brighter hue, similar to a cappuccino, and a less strong yet sweeter taste as opposed to traditional coffee. This beverage is made from the pure root of ginseng, a very ancient plant with numerous virtues.

But be careful: drinking a ginseng coffee isn't necessarily a safe option, as ginseng is not the only ingredient and is present in quite small amounts, quite frequently.

Ginseng Coffee Properties and benefits

Yet let's think about its key advantages and properties before we discover what's in a cup of this beverage:

- Products are energizing. This is, after all, one of the key factors that drive this espresso substitute's use. This decreases tension and tiredness, offers higher energy and increases physical strength, while it contains less caffeine than regular coffee.
- It reinforces brain function. It especially benefits mnemonic capabilities and concentration.
- Improves circulation, and reduces cholesterol. In ginseng, the active substances activate the

physiological mechanism by which our body generates energy, burning sugar and fat.
- Favour digestion—a classic coffee characteristic which is also present in the Asian spice variety.

Which is in a cup of coffee with ginseng?

There are different varieties of ginseng coffee on the market, many of which, unfortunately, are of poor quality. The main ingredients are:

- Sugar (A sour taste of the ginseng roots).
- Bottled coffee.
- Ginseng extract

Sugar is present in large concentrations in the less safe forms, and the ginseng extract is substituted with ginseng fragrance. Not only that, but it also adds the following elements:

- Vegetable cream
- Flavourings.
- Milk cream
- We have hydrogenated vegetable fat.
- Food colourings

How to make homemade ginseng coffee

It is simple, quick to prepare ginseng coffee at home and helps you to avoid unhealthy solutions without forgetting your particular taste.

Materials

- Half a spoonful of dry root ginseng extract (available in any herbal shop).

- A caffee ristretto (about 20 ml).
- 70 ml warm and non-boiling milk.
- Good taste of sugar.

Preparation

1. Heat the milk, without bringing it to boil.
2. Add an extract from the ginseng root.
3. Then stir the coffee along with everything.
4. Finally, add sugar if you wish.

Your homemade ginseng coffee is ready in no time! Click here to learn more about chicory coffee and barley coffee if you are looking for an alternative to classic espresso: no caffeine but a lot of taste and many health benefits.

7 PROVEN BENEFITS OF GINSENG

Ginseng has been used for decades in traditional Chinese medicine.

There are three ways to describe this slow-growing, small plant with fleshy roots, depending on how long it is grown: young, white or red.

New ginseng is harvested for four years, white ginseng is harvested for 4–6 years, and red ginseng is harvested for six years or more.

There are several varieties of this herb, but American ginseng (Panax quinquefolius) and Asian ginseng (Panax ginseng) are the most common.

American and Asian ginseng are variable in their concentration of active compounds and body effects. American ginseng is believed to act as a calming agent, while Asian variety has a boosting effect.

Ginseng has two major compounds: ginsenosides and gintonine. These compounds complement each other to give health benefits

Below are seven evidentiary health benefits of ginseng.

1. Efficient antioxidant to reduce inflammation

Ginseng has positive antioxidant and flame retardant properties. Some test-tube studies have demonstrated that ginseng extracts and ginsenoside compounds can inhibit inflammation and increase the potential for antioxidants in cells.

One test-tube research, for example, found that Korean red ginseng extract reduced inflammation and enhanced antioxidant activity are skin cells from people with eczema. The results, too, are promising in humans.

One research studied the results of making 18 young male athletes spend seven days, taking 2 grams of Korean red ginseng extract three times a day. After performing an exercise test, the men then had levels of certain inflammatory markers tested. Such levels were considerably lower than in the placebo community and lasted up to 72 hours after testing

It should be remembered, however, that the placebo group has a specific medicinal herb, so it is important to take these findings with a grain of salt and further tests. Finally, a larger study tracked 71 postmenopausal women who spent 12 weeks taking 3 grams of red ginseng or a placebo every day. It then assessed the antioxidant activity and the oxidative stress markers.

Researchers concluded that red ginseng would help reduce oxidant stress by increasing the activity of antioxidant enzymes

It has been demonstrated that ginseng helps to reduce inflammatory markers and protect against oxidative stress.

2. Can be helpful for brain function

Ginseng might help improve functions of the brain, such as memory, behaviour and mood. Many test-tube and animal studies indicate that components in ginseng, such as ginsenosides and compound K, may protect the brain from free radicals causing damage.

One study tracked 30 stable people, who for four weeks ate 200 mg of Panax ginseng daily. We had demonstrated progress in mental health, social functioning, and mood at the end of the study. However, after eight weeks, these benefits stopped being significant, suggesting that ginseng effects could diminish with extended use.

Another study examined how single doses of Panax ginseng, either 200 or 400 mg, were taken before and after a 10-minute mental test affected mental performance, mental fatigue and blood sugar levels in 30 healthy adults.

Like the 400-mg dose, the 200-mg dose has been more effective in enhancing mental efficiency and fatigue during the study. Ginseng could have helped cells consume blood sugar, which may have increased efficiency and reduced mental exhaustion. And why the lower dose was more effective than, the higher, is not clear.

A third study found that eight days of taking 400 mg of Panax ginseng a day improved calmness and math skills. What's more, other research finds beneficial effects in people with Alzheimer's disease on brain activity and behaviour.

Ginseng has been shown to support both healthy people and those with Alzheimer's disease from mental processes, feelings of calmness and mood.

3. Could improve Erectile Dysfunction

Research has shown that ginseng can be a useful option for treating men with erectile dysfunction (ED). It may seem that compounds in it can protect the blood vessels and tissues of the penis against oxidative stress and help restore normal function.

Additionally, studies have shown that ginseng can encourage the production of nitric oxide, a compound that enhances the relaxation of the penile muscle and increases circulation of the blood.

One study found that men treated with Korean red ginseng had an improvement of 60% in symptoms of ED compared to an improvement of 30% with a drug used to treat ED

Additionally, another study found that 86 men with ED had significant improvements in erectile function and overall satisfaction after eight weeks of taking 1,000 mg of aged ginseng extract

However, it takes more studies to draw definite conclusions on the effects of ginseng on ED. Ginseng may improve erectile dysfunction symptoms by decreasing oxidative stress in tissues and increasing blood flow in penile muscles.

4. Can make the immune system stronger

Ginseng will strengthen the immune system.

Many research exploring its effects on the immune system have focused on cancer patients undergoing surgery or treatment with chemotherapy. One study followed 39 people recovering from the surgery for stomach cancer, treating them for two years with 5,400 mg of ginseng daily. Interestingly, Those individuals experienced significant increases in immune function and lower recurrence of symptoms.

Another research investigated the effect of red ginseng extract on immune system markers in persons undergoing postoperative chemotherapy with advanced stomach cancer.

Anyone who took red ginseng extract had stronger markers on the immune system than anyone in the control or placebo category after three months. Also, a study suggested that people taking ginseng may have up to a 35 per cent higher chance of living disease-free for five years after curative surgery and up to a 38 per cent higher rate of survival compared to those who do not.

It would appear that ginseng extract could also improve the impact of vaccines on diseases such as influenza.

Although these studies indicate changes in markers of the immune system in people with cancer, further work is needed to demonstrate the effectiveness of ginseng in improving healthy people's resistance to infections. In people with cancer, ginseng may improve the immune system and may even increase the effectiveness of some vaccinations.

5. Will have possible Cancer benefits

Ginseng may help to lower the risk of certain cancers.

In this herb, ginsenosides have been shown to help minimize inflammation and provide protection against antioxidants.

The cell cycle is the mechanism by which cells develop and divide in the usual way. Ginsenosides may benefit from this process by preventing the development and growth of abnormal cells. An analysis of several studies found that people taking ginseng could have a 16 per cent lower cancer risk.

Also, an observational study indicated that people who take ginseng might be less likely to develop certain forms of cancer, such as tongue, mouth, oesophagus, stomach, prostate, liver and lung cancer, than those who do not.

Ginseng can also contribute to improving the health of patients receiving chemotherapy, minimizing side effects, and enhancing the efficacy of certain medications.

Although studies of ginseng's function in cancer prevention reveal some benefits, they remain inconclusive. Ginsenosides in ginseng tend to control inflammation, provide antioxidant protection and preserve cell health which may help to reduce the risk of some forms of cancer. Nevertheless, there is a need for further research.

6. May combat fatigue and increase energy levels

Ginseng has been shown to help counter tiredness and to encourage strength.

Different animal studies have linked some of the components in ginseng, such as polysaccharides and oligopeptides, with lower oxidative stress and higher cell energy output that could help combat fatigue.

One four-week research studied the impact of providing 1 or 2 grams of Panax ginseng or placebo to 90 chronically fatigued people.

Those with Panax ginseng had less physical and mental exhaustion than those taking placebo and less oxidative stress.

The research has provided 364 survivors of cancer fatigued with 2,000 mg of American ginseng or placebo. Eight weeks later, those in the ginseng group reported substantially lower fatigue rates than those in the placebo group. Also, a study of more than 155 studies indicated that ginseng supplements could not only help minimize fatigue but also increase physical activity.

Ginseng can help combat fatigue and increase physical activity by reducing oxidizing damage and increasing cell energy output.

7. Can Lower Blood Sugar

Ginseng tends to be effective in regulating blood glucose in both diabetic and nondiabetic people.

American and Asian ginseng has been shown to improve the function of pancreatic cells, boost insulin production and increase blood sugar uptake in tissues. Also, studies show that ginseng extracts help by providing antioxidant protection which reduces free radicals in those with diabetes cells.

One study evaluated the effects of 6 grams of Korean red ginseng, in 19 people with type 2 diabetes, along with the usual anti-diabetic medication or diet.

Interestingly, during the 12-week study, they managed to maintain good blood sugar control. They also had an 11 per cent reduction in blood sugar levels, a 38 per cent reduction in fasting insulin, and an insulin sensitivity rise of 33 per cent.

Another study has shown that American ginseng helped improve blood sugar levels in 10 healthy people after a sugar beverage test.

It would seem that fermented red ginseng could be even more efficient at regulating blood sugar. With the help of live bacteria, fermented ginseng is produced, which transforms the ginsenosides into a more easily absorbed and potent form. Yes, a study found that taking 2.7 grams of fermented red ginseng daily was effective in lowering blood sugar and rising levels of insulin after a test meal compared to placebo.

Ginseng, especially fermented red ginseng, may help increase insulin output, increase blood sugar intake in cells, and provide protection against antioxidants.

Simple to integrate into your diet

The root ginseng can be eaten in many ways. You can eat it raw, or you can steam it gently to soften it.

To make a tea, it can be stewed in water too. To do this, simply add hot water to freshly sliced ginseng and allow it to steep for a few minutes.

Ginseng can also be added to different recipes such as soups, and stir-frys. And the extract can be used in types of powder, tablet, capsule, and liquid.

How much to take depends on the condition that you wish to improve. Overall, daily doses of 1–2 grams of raw ginseng root or an extract of 200–400 mg are recommended. Starting with lower doses is best, and rising over time.

Look for a standard ginseng extract containing 2–3 per cent of total ginsenosides, and consume it before meals to increase absorption and get the full benefits.

Ginseng can be eaten fresh, made into a tea or added to a variety of different dishes. This can also be eaten as paste, gel, or liquid.

Health and its potential side effects

Ginseng appears to be healthy according to studies and does not cause any significant adverse effects.

People taking diabetes medications, however, should closely monitor their blood sugar levels when using ginseng to ensure that those levels do not go too low. Additionally, ginseng may decrease anticoagulant drug effectiveness. Speak to the doctor for these reasons before supplementing with it.

Remember that ginseng is not approved for children or women who are pregnant or breastfeeding because of a lack of health studies. Eventually, there is evidence suggesting that prolonged use of ginseng can decrease its efficacy in the body.

To optimize its benefits, ginseng should be taken in periods of 2–3 weeks with a one or two week break in between. Although ginseng seems healthy, people taking other medicines should pay attention to potential interactions with the medication.

Ginseng is a herbal supplement, used in Chinese medicine for decades. It is popularly known for its antioxidant and anti-inflammatory effect. It could also help regulate blood sugar levels and benefit some cancers. Also, ginseng can boost the immune system, enhance brain activity, combat fatigue and improve erectile dysfunction symptoms. Ginseng can be eaten raw or steamed gently. It can also be easily added to your diet through its extract, capsule or type of powder.

Ginseng is worth a try, whether you want to improve a certain condition or simply boost your health.

Chapter 12: ALCOHOL AND CAFFEINE

Irish coffee, Rum and coke, Jagerbombs — all these rising drinks mix alcohol and caffeinated beverages. But, is mixing the two safe?

The short answer is that it is usually not advised to mix caffeine and alcohol, although there are a variety of reasons to bear in mind. Read on for more on the effects of mixing caffeine with alcohol.

Which depends on mixing?

Caffeine is a stimulant which can make you feel vigorous and alert. In comparison, alcohol is a depressant that can make you feel tired or less alert than normal.

When combining a stimulant with a depressant, the stimulant can mask the effects of the depressant. In other words, the combination of caffeine and alcohol may mask some of the depressant effects of alcohol. You will feel more alert and enthusiastic than you would usually be drinking.

BUT, Did NOT SOBER ME UP?

No. No. If you drink some caffeine, you may feel a little more alert, but it won't change your blood alcohol level or the way your body cleans alcohol from your system.

If you do not experience the full effects of alcohol, you are at a higher risk of drinking more than you would normally. This, in turn, increases your risk of other things, including driving while intoxicated, intoxicating alcohol or injuring.

What are the energy drinks?

Energy drinks, including Red Bull, Bear, and Rockstar, are heavily caffeinated beverages. Such beverages also contain other stimulants as well as elevated sugar levels, in addition to caffeine.

For energy drinks, the level of caffeine varies and depends on the medication. According to the Food and Drug Administration (FDA)Trusted Source, the caffeine content of energy drinks can range between 40 and 250 milligrams (mg) per 8 ounces.

The same volume of coffee brewed has between 95 and 165 mg of caffeine, for comparison. It is also important to remember that a lot of energy drinks come in 16-ounce bottles and that the actual amount of caffeine in one energy drink will vary from 80 to 500 mg.

Experts have been looking more closely over the effects of mixing energy drinks with caffeine in recent years. Several studies relate the two to an increased riskTrusted Source of injury and an increased probabilityTrusted Source of binge drinking.

Caffeinated alcoholic beverages

Several firms, including Four Loko and Joose, started introducing caffeine and other stimulants to their alcoholic drinks in the early 2000s. These beverages also had a higher alcohol content than beer, in addition to the high levels of caffeine.

In 2010, the FDA issued a Trusted Source warning to four firms that made such beverages, claiming the caffeine in the drinks was an unhealthy food additive. The companies removed caffeine and other stimulants from certain goods in response to this comment.

What other sources of caffeine?

Although it is never recommended to combine alcohol and caffeine, some combinations of the two could be less risky than others. Note, the biggest issue is that caffeine will mask the alcohol effects, causing you to drink more than you would normally do.

But what about drinks which are not as caffeinated as energy drinks? There's still the risk, but it's not quite as high.

A rum and coke made from one single shot of rum contain 30 to 40 mg of caffeine for the context. Meanwhile, a Red Bull with a single shot of vodka could contain 80 to 160 mg of caffeine — potentially more than three times as much caffeine as usual.

Although you should usually avoid mixing alcohol and caffeine, consuming an Irish coffee on occasion does not hurt you. Only make sure to eat these types of beverages in moderation and be mindful not only of the alcohol content but also the possible content of caffeine.

What if I drink alcohol and caffeine separately?

How about getting an hour or two with a cup of coffee or tea before he reaches the bar? Caffeine will remain in your body for five to six hours, but it diminishes gradually over time.

If within a few hours of consuming alcohol, you ingest caffeine, you also run the risk of not experiencing the full effects of the alcohol you ingest.

You should also bear in mind, though, that the content of caffeine in things like coffee and tea can vary greatly depending on how they are made.

It is not a good idea to drink 16 ounces of cold-brew coffee right before a bar crawl, but an 8-ounce cup of green tea probably won't have too much effect.

If I mix them, are there any symptoms that I should watch out for?

Both alcohol and caffeine are diuretics, and they help you urinate even more. As a result, the mixing of caffeine and alcohol may be a problem for dehydration.

Such signs of dehydration to watch out for include:

- feeling thirsty
- passing dark urine
- having a dry mouth
- feeling dizzy or lightheaded

The biggest thing to look out for, though, is to drink too much, which at best can lead to a bad hangover, and at worst to alcohol poisoning.

RECOGNIZING POISONING ALCOHOL

Some symptoms of alcohol poisoning to be aware of are:

- Feeling disoriented or confused
- being conscious but not responsive
- severe loss of coordination
- seizures
- vomiting
- slowed breathing (less than eight breaths in a minute)
- irregular breathing (more than 10 seconds pass between breaths)
- slowed heart rate
- difficulty staying conscious
- clammy or pale skin

- passing out and being difficult to wake up

Alcohol poisoning is also an emergency and requires hospital care. If you think someone has alcohol poisoning, you should always seek emergency medical attention.

Chapter 13: THE COLD BREW

Cold brewing, dripping or espresso, some kind of brewed coffee in moderation is perfect for us. Drinking coffee offers various health benefits. Coffee can enhance athletic efficiency, minimize the risk of diabetes, colon cancer, gallstones and Parkinson's disease, as well as improve liver health. However, cold brew is especially beneficial to our health while reducing some of the side effects associated with coffee consumption.

This is because the coffee, brewed with cold water, has a different chemical profile. I am not saying that if your body agrees with it, you will stop drinking your espresso every day. Nevertheless, the cold brew will satisfy the caffeine craving, and the tasty no-calorie drink, in a healthier way. Let us see how different the cold brew is from the steam brewed coffee.

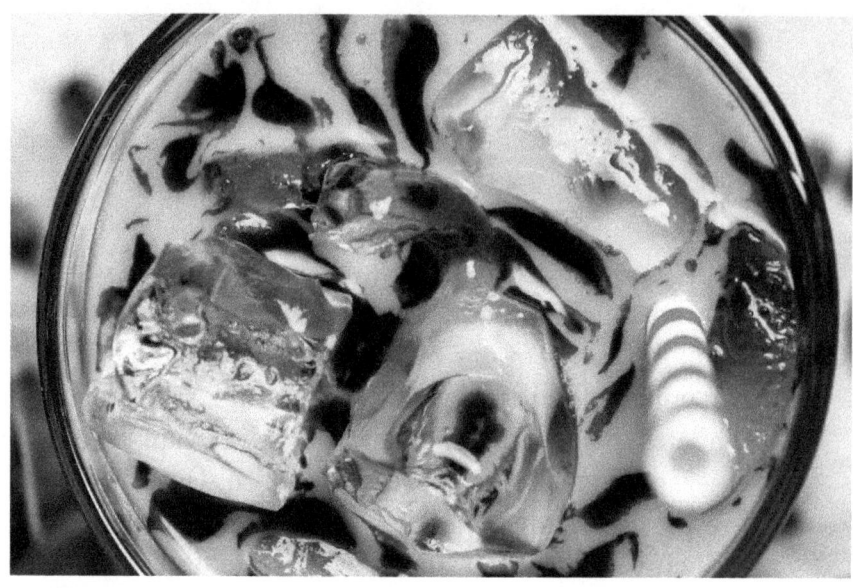

Health benefits of cold brew coffee

Believe it or not, coffee is one of the planet's healthiest beverages. No, not the coffee from your Starbuck packed with an unknown amount of artificial sweeteners and flavourings; but genuine coffee. You may want to look at cold brew health benefits to take your coffee drinking to the next level for those of you who at least appreciate the benefits of drinking coffee safely!

To those of you who can drink traditional hot coffee without any ill-effects, you would certainly still benefit from switching to cold brew. But particularly for those people who encounter stomach problems when they drink hot coffee, cold brew coffee may be a surprising advantages

Many health benefits are attributed to drinking cold brew coffee, but marketing distorts the facts that exaggerate some of the facts. Here are the health benefits of cold brew that are discussed most:

Cold Brew is a strong antioxidant – contains more chlorogenic acid

Hot brewed coffee contains 40 mg of caffeine per 100 grams and no substantial amount of essential nutrients. From this perspective, Cold Brew Coffee is very similar to Drip. That is where similitudes end, though.

Recent nutritional discoveries show how important phytonutrients are for our health. As a result, green coffee is a big source of phytochemicals and is a perfect antioxidant. However, exposure to high temperatures destroys the antioxidants; the higher the temperature, and the longer the exposure, the more antioxidants are destroyed. At low temperatures, processed coffee retains a higher antioxidant ratio.

Chlorogenic acid is a strong antioxidant found in coffee beans, but it is extremely heat sensitive. Chlorogenic acid itself is a justification for you to drink coffee every day, but roasting the coffee beans is harmful to this incredible antioxidant 's health.

Light roast coffee can post a chlorogenic acid breakdown of up to 60%, while darker roasts can break down to 100%! This is an incredibly huge loss to your overall coffee wellbeing because it is a widely accepted aim of science to increase the amount of this substance in each cup of coffee one day.

The only trade-off with cold brew is that some of the terpenes in coffee (aromatic oils) are the basis for the aromas and coffee taste. Because the terpenes need heat to be drained from the grounds, the cold brew does not have the same kick as the hot brew.

Therefore we have not all turned to cold brew yet. However, once you try a cup of cold brew, its complex aroma and taste will amaze you. Cold brew coffee has a delicate, unique flavour.

It is described by people as sweet, with floral, earthy notes and no bitterness. You don't need any sugar, and it's very mild in taste.

The same work previously described calculated the number of antioxidants in the coffee. Their results supported earlier work that cold brew retains chlorogenic acid better. Nonetheless, the article writers Niny Rao and Megan Fuller find a higher antioxidant potential in a hot brew.

That is because the coffee absorbs other antioxidant compounds at higher temperatures.

Caffeine content

I love a good espresso. But even in the afternoon, I enjoy my espresso. However, because of the caffeine, many people can not have a second cup. Many people don't even respond with massive quantities of caffeine, but just a drink over the normal dose of coffee may lead to serious problems for others. Also, without an obvious reaction, high doses of caffeine may contribute to serious conditions such as osteoporosis, anxiety, depression, sleep disorders and many other issues. Here's a report about this from N.I.H.

The cold brew coffee contains about 40 milligrams of coffee per 100 grams. That is 20 milligrams less than your coffee shop 's regular drip coffee. Sure, for the energy jolt, many people only drink coffee. I drink it for fun, and I want to drink some of it, without too much caffeine consumed. If your afternoon drink needs to be even less caffeinated then mixing it with chicory is the best choice. You get a strong coffee this way, without the caffeine. My favourite afternoon beverage is cold brew coffee and chicory. Here's my chicory-coffee story.

Extraction of caffeine may be improved by steeping for longer.

CHOLESTEROL AND COLD BREW
There are a few studies that show that unfiltered coffee intake can influence the development of cholesterol. Kahweol and cafestol are two molecules responsible for increasing LDL cholesterol. This has been scientifically verified and discussed here by JRSM.

I don't care much about coffee-raised LDL cholesterol although I'm a health nut. But that is another argument. Anyway, going back to the subject, cold brew is assumed to contain less kahweol and cafestol due to the low temperature of the brewing.

There is no scientific research on the subject; it's only presumed that at higher temperatures, the two terpenes are better extracted. If you want to make sure you don't have them in your coffee, just filter them. Oh, and make sure that your grinder is a decent one, so your field is standard. Fines will pass both of these compounds to your cup.

Review of health benefits of cold brew

If you're one of the millions of people avidly beginning their day with a cup of energy and warning coffee, it's smart to remember how you're serving your coffee.

If you've tried drinking dark roast coffee, and still can't control your stomach problems, cold brew coffee is the right drink for you! Cold-brew has lower acid content, but that does not mean much for your wellbeing. The many facets of cold brew nutrition should be enough to at least try it out!

Cold-brew coffee will give you more of the strong chlorogenic acid antioxidant while hot brew will give you other antioxidants.

9 IMPRESSIVE COLD-BREW COFFEE BENEFITS

In recent years, cold brew coffee has risen to prominence among coffee drinkers.

Instead of using hot water to extract the flavour and caffeine from coffee beans, cold brew coffee relies on time by steeping them for 12–24 hours in cold water.

This way, the drink is less sour than hot coffee.

While most work on coffee's health benefits uses a hot brew, it is thought that cold brew provides several similar effects.

The cold brew coffee has nine amazing health benefits here.

1. Can boost metabolism

Metabolism is the mechanism by which the body makes use of food to produce energy.

The higher the metabolic rate, the higher the calories you burn while you rest.

Like hot coffee, cold brew coffee contains caffeine that has been shown to increase the rate of metabolic rest by up to 11%

Caffeine tends to improve the metabolic rate by increasing the speed at which the body burns fat.

In a study of 8 people, ingestion of caffeine resulted in a 13 per cent increase in calorie burning, as well as a 2-fold increase in fat-burning — much greater effects than they had after taking a placebo or beta-blocker (medication for blood pressure and circulation)

Caffeine in cold brew coffee will increase the number of calories you burn when you are in rest. That may make weight loss or weight retention easier.

2. Might lift your mood

Caffeine in cold brew coffee can improve your mental state.

Consumption of caffeine has been shown to improve mood, especially among sleep-deprived individuals.

An analysis of research of more than 370,000 people showed lower levels of depression among those who drank coffee. Also, the risk of depression decreased by 8 per cent for every cup of coffee consumed per day.

Some work has also indicated that caffeine could be used as a dietary supplement in older adults to improve mood and brain function.

In a study conducted in 12 adults aged 63–74, taking 1.4 mg of caffeine per pound (3 mg per kg) improved mood by 17 per cent. For the average person, that amount of caffeine is equivalent to around two cups of coffee.

Caffeine has also enhanced their ability to respond to an object that moves toward them, meaning it increases concentration and attention.

Drinking cold brew coffee will increase your mood, decrease your risk of depression and boost brain function.

3. May reduce the risk of cardiac disease

Heart disease is a general term for many conditions that may affect the heart, including heart attack, coronary artery disease, and stroke. It is the number one worldwide cause of death.

Cold brew coffee contains compounds that can reduce heart attack risk, including caffeine, phenolic compounds, magnesium, trigonelline, guides, and lignans. It increases sensitivity to insulin, stabilizes blood sugar and reduces blood pressure.

The drink also includes diterpenes and chlorogenic acids (CGAs), which serve as antioxidants and anti-inflammatory agents.

Drinking 3–5 cups of coffee every day (15–25 ounces or 450–750 ml) will minimize the risk of heart disease by up to 15% compared to people who don't drink coffee.

There is no evidence to indicate that consuming more than 3–5 cups a day raises the risk of heart disease, but this effect has not been observed in people who consume more than 600 mg of caffeine a day, which is the equivalent of around 6 cups of coffee.

People with uncontrolled high blood pressure should actively avoid drinking caffeine, as this can further increase their levels.

Drinking cold brew coffee regularly can improve the health of your heart. However, if you have uncontrolled high blood pressure, caffeine should be restricted or avoided.

4. Will reduce the Type 2 diabetes risk

Type 2 diabetes is a chronic disease where you have too much blood sugar levels. It can lead to many severe health problems if left untreated.

Cold-brew coffee will lower the risk of developing this disease. Drinking at least 4–6 cups of coffee a day is generally associated with a decreased risk of type 2 diabetes

These benefits can be due in large part to chlorogenic acids, which are potent antioxidants in coffee

Cold-brew coffee can also regulate gut peptides, which are hormones that monitor and slow digestion in your digestive system, keeping your blood sugar stable

One analysis of more than 36,900 people aged 45–74 showed that those who drank at least 4 cups of coffee a day had a 30 per cent lower risk of type 2 diabetes than those who did not drink coffee a day.

An analysis of 3 major studies of over 1 million people showed that those who increased their consumption of coffee over four years had an 11% lower risk of type 2 diabetes compared to a 17% higher risk of those who decreased their consumption of coffee by more than 1 cup per day.

Taking cold brew coffee regularly will help regulate your blood sugar and reduce the risk of type 2 diabetes.

5. Could reduce the risk of Alzheimer's and Parkinson 's disease

In addition to increasing your mindfulness and mood, cold brew coffee may otherwise benefit your brain.

Caffeine stimulates your nervous system and may affect the workings of your brain.

One recent study found that coffee drinking would protect the brain against age-related illnesses.

Alzheimer's and Parkinson's diseases are neurodegenerative conditions, meaning they are caused by long-term brain cell death. Both diseases can lead to dementia, a deterioration in mental health that hampers daily activities.

Alzheimer's disease is characterized by significant memory impairment, whereas Parkinson's frequently causes physical tremors and rigidity.

One retrospective study suggested that participants who drank 3–5 cups of coffee a day in the middle of their lives had a 65 per cent lower risk of developing dementia and Alzheimer's in old age

Another observational study found that there is a lower risk of Parkinson's disease among coffee drinkers. People who drink more than four cups of coffee a day are reportedly five times less likely to develop this condition.

Several coffee compounds, such as phenylindanes, as well as harmful and non-Harman compounds, tend to offer defence against Alzheimer's and Parkinson 's disease.

Note that decaffeinated coffee does not appear to deliver the same safety advantages as caffeinated varieties (22).

Cold brew coffee contains phenylindane compounds and lower levels of nonharman and Harman compounds. This will help protect the brain from diseases associated with ageing.

6. Might be better on the stomach than hot coffee

Many people avoid coffee, as it is an acidic drink that can induce reflux of acid.

Acid reflux is a disorder in which the stomach acid often flows back into the oesophagus and induces discomfort

Coffee acidity often appears to be blamed for other illnesses, for example, indigestion and heartburn.

The pH scale tests how acidic or alkaline a solution ranges from 0 to 14, with seven being neutral, lower numbers being more acidic and higher alkaline numbers.

Cold-brew and hot coffee typically have similar levels of acidity on the pH scale, about 5–6, but this can differ depending on the individual brews.

Also, some studies have shown that cold brew is slightly less acidic, which means your stomach may get less irritated.

Another reason this drink may be less annoying than hot coffee is its crude polysaccharide content.

Such carbohydrates, or molecular sugar chains, strengthen the digestive system's immune system. This may minimize inflammation of the gut and the unpleasant effects of the acidity of the coffee on your stomach.

Cold brew coffee is just marginally less acidic than hot coffee but contains compounds that can protect the stomach from the acidity. As such, it can cause fewer symptoms of disagreeable digestive and acid reflux than hot coffee.

7. Will help you carry on living longer

Drinking cold brew coffee can reduce your overall risk of death, as well as dying from specific causes of the disease.

A long-term study of 229,119 men and 173,141 women between the ages of 50–71 found that the more coffee people drink, the lower the risk of death from heart disease, respiratory disease, stroke, injury, accidents, diabetes and infections.

Coffee is rich in antioxidants, may be one explanation for this association.

Antioxidants are substances that help avoid damage to the cells that can lead to chronic diseases such as heart disease, type 2 diabetes and cancer. Those conditions will shorten your lifespan significantly.

Coffee contains powerful antioxidants such as polyphenols, chlorogenic acid and hydroxycinnamates.

Although studies show that hot coffee contains more total antioxidants than cold brew types, the latter packs some very potent antioxidants, including caffeoylquinic acid (CQA) for example.

Though cold brew coffee contains less total antioxidants than hot coffee, it is full of high antioxidant activity compounds. Antioxidants help avoid diseases that may decrease your lifespan.

8. Caffeine content similar to that of hot coffee. Cold brew coffee is produced as a concentrate to be diluted with water, typically in a ratio of 1:1.

On their own, the concentrates are extremely solid. Undiluted, it generally provides about 200 mg of caffeine per cup.

However, diluting the concentrate-as normal-decreases the final product's caffeine content, making it closer to that of standard coffee. Although the content of caffeine can vary depending on the method of brewing, the difference in caffeine content between hot coffee and cold brew is negligible.

The average hot coffee cup contains about 95 mg of caffeine, compared to about 100 mg for a standard cold brew.

Hot coffee and cold brew contain equal levels of caffeine. However, it would have about twice the caffeine if you drank cold brew coffee concentrate without diluting it.

9. Quite easy to make

Cold-brew coffee can be made easily at home.

1. Next, buy whole roasted coffee beans locally or online, then grind them roughly.
2. Add 8 ounces of grounds (226 grams) to a large jar and stir gently in 2 cups (480 ml) of water.
3. Cover the container and let the coffee steep for 12–24 hours in the refrigerator.
4. Place the cheesecloth in a fine mesh strainer and pour into another jar the steeped coffee through.
5. The solids that collect on the cheesecloth are discarded or saved for other creative uses. The remaining liquid is a concentrate of your cold brew coffee.
6. Cover the jar with an airtight lid, and store your concentrate for up to two weeks in the fridge.
7. Connect 1/2 cup (120 ml) of cold water to 1/2 cup (120 ml) of cold brew coffee concentrate when you're ready to drink. Pour over ice, then add cream if desired.

It takes a much longer time to prepare cold brew coffee than hot coffee, this makes it really simple at home. Mix coarse ground coffee beans with cold water, leave to steep for 12–24 hours, strain, then dilute the concentrate at 1:1 ratio.

Cold brew coffee is a good alternative to the hot coffee you can make easily at home.

This provides many of the same health benefits but is less acidic and less salty, which can make it easier for sensitive individuals to handle.

If you want to mix your coffee routine, try cold brew coffee and see how it is comparable to your usual hot joe cup.

Is Cold Brew better than Ordinary?

Nitro coffee has been turning up in both coffee shops and grocery stores in the years after its launch.

This uniquely cold-brewed style of coffee is infused with nitrogen gas to enhance both taste and texture. It is served directly from the tap as opposed to standard coffee and is enjoyed cold rather than hot piping.

Standard coffee is also believed to be superior, both in terms of taste and texture, and the health benefits it offers.

The main differences and similarities between nitro coffee and standard coffee are discussed here.

Thicker Texture

Nitro coffee provides a dense, creamy texture that separates it from standard coffee.

Similar to other drinks, such as sparkling water or soda, nitro coffee is infused with small bubbles of gas which alter the mouthfeel.

While these other drinks are made using carbon dioxide, however, nitro coffee is infused with nitrogen.

This gives it a frothy, foam-like appearance and a smooth mouth-feel sometimes contrasted with beer.

In nitro coffee, therefore, ingredients used to improve the flavour of regular coffee — such as milk or creamer — are not usually available.

Infused with nitrogen, nitro coffee gives it a foamy appearance and a smooth mouthfeel.

Sweeter Tastes

Besides improving your cup of coffee's texture and mouth-feel, the nitrogen used in nitro coffee also adds a hint of sweetness.

What's more, ground and brewed cold coffee, such as nitro coffee, has been shown to have increased aroma and flavour.

This effect makes nitro a good alternative to standard coffee for many, as it makes extra sugar unnecessary.

Not only can added sugar raise your coffee's calorie content and eventually result in weight gain, but consuming too much sugar has also been associated with a host of long-term health issues.

Also, studies show that eating large levels of added sugar can be associated with an increased risk of heart disease, type 2 diabetes, and even cancer of some forms.

When you're usually adding sugar to your coffee, nitro coffee may be a healthy option to help you reduce your sugar intake and prevent such negative health effects.

Nitro coffee has a sweeter flavour than standard coffee and needs no added sugar, which can help to minimize calories. Diets high in sugar have been linked to heart disease, diabetes and cancer.

Less Acidic

One of the main differences between nitro and standard coffee is their respective acidity levels.

Many of the acids present in daily coffee show up only at 195–205 ° F (90–96 ° C) higher temperatures.

Hence, brewing nitro coffee at a lower temperature can result in considerably less acidity than regular coffee.

Some people may find this mildness particularly helpful, as the acids found in coffee may irritate your stomach and cause digestive problems.

The low acid count also produces a special taste and reduces nitro coffee bitterness.

Cold-brewed coffee, however, can have less beneficial compounds like chlorogenic acid, an antioxidant that provides much of the acidity in a standard coffee.

Yes, evidence indicates that chlorogenic acid can have anti-inflammatory, anti-diabetic, and anti-cancer effects and can help prevent chronic illnesses.

Nitro coffee has a lower acidity than standard coffee, which may reduce the risk of malaise in the stomach. It can also be lower in beneficial antioxidants, like chlorogenic acid, however.

Higher in Caffeine

Nitro coffee is made using a higher ratio of coffee grounds to water than regular coffee and is capable of absorbing the caffeine content.

Some firms also say that nitro coffee boasts more than 30 per cent more caffeine per ounce (30 ml) per ounce than standard coffee, though rates may differ by the maker.

Caffeine has been associated with several health benefits, with some studies suggesting that consumption of caffeine is associated with improved metabolism, improved athletic success and a decreased risk of type 2 diabetes.

That being said, nitro coffee's higher caffeine content might not help everyone.

Caffeine is not only highly addictive, but it can also cause side effects such as anxiety, irregular heartbeat, headaches and high blood pressure.

Some evidence indicates that certain individuals may be more prone to the effects of caffeine and may be more likely to encounter adverse effects because of variations in genetics.

Nitro coffee comes with a higher level of caffeine than standard coffee. Although caffeine can give some health benefits, it can also cause some side effects in sensitive people.

Same health benefits as daily coffee

The health benefits of standard and nitro coffee, if it comes down to it, are very similar.

Both contain caffeine, antioxidants and a host of essential micronutrients — like riboflavin and pantothenic acid — for your health (13).

Additionally, regular coffee is linked to a long list of health benefits:

- Depression decreases: consuming at least four cups of coffee a day will minimize the risk of depression by up to 20 per cent
- Improves longevity: studies have linked coffee intake to lower death risk.
- Decreases risk of diabetes: daily coffee intake was associated with a lower risk of type 2 diabetes of 30–35 per cent.
- Dementia protection: increased consumption of caffeine may be associated with lower dementia risk, as well as Alzheimer's and Parkinson's risk.
- Aids weight loss: The intake of caffeine has been shown to improve metabolism and ramp up fat burning to improve weight loss

While nitro coffee's particular effects have not been thoroughly studied, it is made from the same ingredients as regular coffee. It is likely to share a similar set of health attributes.

Nitro coffee and standard coffee share the same ingredients and have similar health benefits likely to be received. Coffee has been linked with many beneficial effects on health, from improved metabolism to lower diabetes risk.

How to Home Make It

For its distinctive taste and texture, Nitro coffee is a common choice among coffee lovers.

Unfortunately, it can be difficult to find and is often expensive — about $3–5 for a single cup.

While making true nitro coffee requires additional equipment to infuse nitrogen into the coffee, for a similar taste and nutrient profile, you can try making a batch of cold brew coffee at home:

1. Combine 4 ounces (57 grams) of coarse ground coffee with around 4 cups of water (946 millilitres). Then just swirl and relax for 18–24 hours.
2. Offer is over a strainer and cheesecloth to separate the coffee grounds from the coffee concentrates after the coffee has stopped steeping.
3. Move the drink into a clean glass, and enjoy it.

You can change the quantities to produce larger amounts and store the drink in the fridge for up to two weeks at a time.

Although additional equipment is needed to make true nitro coffee, using only a few ingredients, you can easily make cold brew coffee in the home.

Cold-brewed nitro coffee tastes sweeter than standard coffee and has a thicker and smoother texture.

What's more, the caffeine becomes less acidic and higher.

Nevertheless, standard and nitro coffee is a close match when it comes to nutritional value and health benefits, such as weight loss and increased lifespan.

Feel free to turn off your hot cup of coffee from time to time for a cold brew so you can take advantage of the special taste and texture that each has to offer.

Chapter 14: ARABICA COFFEE

Ever wondered why everybody's thinking about Arabica coffee? This label is so prominent that many can't even name any other type of coffee beans. And these same people do not seem to think that much about it anyway. So, what is that little bean deal? Is it Arab? Arabian? What exactly does the word "Arabica" mean and what does that mean to the coffee you drink?

The history of this wonderful little bean in what is now known as modern-day Ethiopia brings us back to about the 12th century. Way up in the mountains, it was there that the very first varieties of this bean were cultivated. The story goes it was a goat farmer who began growing the beans and harvesting them. We can't tell for sure whether it started like that, or not. What we do know, though, is that this coffee bean did not take long to take over the world.

Arabica coffee accounts for about 60 per cent of the total global supply of coffee. Yet back to the lesson of our history! So, when this bean went global in the 16th century (or as global as the 16th century) After the Ottoman Empire invaded this region of the world known as the Arabian Peninsula, this new beverage was called the "Wine of Arabia" — thereby laying the foundations for what we now know as Arabica coffee. It continued its journey through the Venetian traders to Europe and was soon a staple in much of the modern world of the 16th century.

This wasn't lost on Ethiopia, which quickly made sure to secure their hold on the coffee market by making exporting the plants illegal. So, of course, as soon as you make doing something illegally, someone would try to do something even more. Eventually, the Dutch stole the plants and smuggled them out of the country. From that moment on, this has contributed to the growth of arabica coffee beans from Indonesia to South America all over the world. Naturally, the downside to that was the denigration of the plant's pure genetic code.

So, that was how it all began and why beans from arabica are so highly desired. But now, where are we? There's more to the modern world today than just the Arabica bean.

We prefer to learn of two types of coffee beans:

Robusta and Arabica.

Two separate species and after the history as mentioned above lesson, it is easy to find out the species is of lesser quality.

Both Robusta and Arabica are cultivated, roasted, and coffee-brewed, but vary in taste and consistency. Think of low grade versus high-grade coffee beans the nearby diner at the corner versus a speciality coffee shop brand.

BETWEEN DIFFERENCES THE BEANS

Let's think about taste first. The flavours of Robusta vary from neutral to strong, and a nut-based aroma can be detected before roasting. However, arabicas have a variety of tastes, from sweet to sharp and even tangy. Unroasted, they smell like blueberries, which, during roasting, makes for a sweet-smelling fruit.

Then there are the differences in farming!

Robusta beans come from a hardy, pest-resistant plant that can multiply in many different areas, as well as at low altitudes. This makes it easy for them to farm and you guessed that, cheap.

On the other side, Arabica is a delicate and slower-growing herb. It only grows in dry, subtropical climates at high altitudes, requires fertile, moist soil and many other specificities for it to become. The elevation is one of the most critical factors that will yield Arabica beans while growing the plants. It usually means an altitude of between 800 and 2200 metres. The flavour is more nuanced and the slower the plant production, depending on the height. All of that helps in the creation of a quality product.

It is essential to note the reason the Robusta plants are so resistant to pests. It turns out; this is due to their higher levels of caffeine and acidity. The Robusta is also a cross-pollinating plant, resulting in more significant variations between the beans and, eventually, the flavours. At the same time, the Arabica is a self-pollinating plant that finally allows more stable bean development to begin.

As in other items, the better the quality that the product is, the more special care required to generate the product. The same is true for beans made from coffee. Arabica started as the best coffee bean the world had seen and is still the highest quality coffee bean on the market today. That's why gourmet coffees are produced almost always from top quality Arabica coffee beans. Many of those quality beans include coffee beans from Honduras, Costa Rica, Guatemala, Ethiopia, and Jamaica 's blue mountains - but more about where they can later be found.

ABOUT THE BEANS
Coffee beans do not begin as beans. They start like many other foods growing on trees-as a fruit. Also, the coffee bean is inside the fruit-which is called the coffee cherry.

Ever wonder why a great coffee always goes well with a sweet treat like chocolate or nuts? That's because the flavours in those delicious treatments imitate the natural flavours in the arabica coffee of high quality. These gourmet coffee beans, like chocolate, nuts, berries and even caramel, often have a slightly sweet taste to them.

Interestingly enough, the beans are the fruit seeds and are found inside the cherries which grow on the plant of Arabica. Harvesting is done when dark red or purple is in the cherry. Usually, a berry has two beans, and they are coated in a thin coating which must be removed before further processing.

WHY ARE BEANS ARABICA FARMED TODAY?

The best places for farming Arabica coffee beans are the tropical climates around the equator. The best spots on the planet for growing this attractive little bean are pretty much Africa and South America.

Some countries which grow coffee beans from Arabica include:

- Colombia
- Mexico
- Costa Rica
- Ecuador
- Guatemala
- Brazil -do you know that the bulk of today's coffee is farmed and processed in Brazil?
- Rwanda
- Ethiopia -The birthplace of Arabica beans!
- Burundi
- India

ARABICA COFFEE BEANS TYPES

So, we spoke about how coffee beans come in either the perfect premium Arabica beans or the Robusta beans of lower quality. We have outlined why Arabica is the best option, but more still! Did you know that Arabica beans are many different kinds of?

Twenty-one varieties are listed for you in alphabetic order. Can this list help you to get a little better understanding of your beans!

1. Typical-A sweet, clean taste. One of the first cultivated plants.
2. Bourbon -no alcohol connection, but instead it boasts a kick of fruity chocolate.
3. Caturra-a bourbon variant but with a lighter citric flavour.
4. Catimor -a fourth Robusta, mellow in flavour.
5. Catuai-tangy one portion, and sweet the other.
6. Gesha-one of the largest and most expensive coffees in the world. Has undertones of flowers and tropical fruits.
7. Jackson -delicate and acidic, even a little edgy.
8. Jamaican Blue Mountain-light, smooth, creamy and a little spicy. Black was also quickly enjoyed.
9. Jember-rich and heavy. At the same time buttery and spice.
10. Kent-delicate and spicy floral, flavours.
11. 11. Kona -some of the costliest coffees in the world. Grown-up between Hawaiian volcanoes. Light and spicy, with underlying spice and nut flavours.

12. Maragogypw-heavy and buttery, with citrus and floral hints
13. . Maracatu / Maracaturra-a crossbreed with a fruity flavour.
14. The Mocca-the name says it all ... Flavoured with chocolate!
15. Mundo nova-another hybrid with a touch of mild caramel sweetness which is a biter.
16. Pacamara-acid sweetness
17. Pacas — sweet and spicy with floral tips.
18. Pache-a typical smooth blend of flats.
19. SL-34 & SL-28 -a more scientific name but also a fruity wine-based flavour called "blueberry bombs."
20. Villa Sarchi-medium body with a distinct taste of berries.
21. Villalobos – a perfect mixture of sweetness and acidity, excellent to drink dry.

So, what is the most critical takeaway for the average regular coffee drinker after all that knowledge about arabica coffee beans? If nothing else is preserved from this article, be it that you want only Arabica beans for your coffee! This doesn't make you a snobbish coffee but rather a well-educated coffee fan! Arabica beans are the best quality on the market, with the most delicious tasting and all-around premium coffee beans. Your body and your coffee deserve nothing less!

Chapter 15: CONCLUSION

Caffeine is a natural way to do so when you need to stay awake. Caffeine is not toxic, in the form of coffee and tea. By replicating a molecule that binds to the cell receptors, caffeine enters the brain and slows them down, getting you ready for sleep. Caffeine, which resembles this molecule called Adenosine, covers your cell receptors, meaning you are not slowed down by Adenosine (Cunningham, April 1, 2000). Caffeine can never be a substitute for rest. Still, it is a good way to make up for it if you need a fast wake-up drink, which is a possible explanation why the number of adults consuming coffee in the US last year alone increased by 5 per cent (Fernau, April 9, 2013).

Caffeine alone, meaning no sugar soft drinks, energy drinks, sweetened teas, and even coffee, has no health drawback found that can affect the body. Caffeine will do the same, potentially.

Not only is coffee a popular beverage all over the world, but it also has some cultural aspects attached to it. This is more than just a bean or a snack. This is an important part of their daily life for plenty of people. It's only appropriate for devoted coffee drinkers to learn and appreciate a little more about their favourite beverage. After knowing a few important things about this world's favourite beverage, fewer people will ask What's Coffee?

Caffeine can be marketed to the general public because it has several beneficial effects. This, of course, means that the average person who routinely drinks caffeine has nothing to worry about unless they drink it instead of sleeping because then they have to deal with sleep deprivation consequences. With that being said, caffeine is a natural pick-me-up that puts you in a better mood and makes you more alert, so don't just sit down there. Get out there and have a cup of coffee!

CPSIA information can be obtained
at www.ICGtesting.com
Printed in the USA
BVHW060257200321
603031BV00006B/1148